BE AMAZING OR GO HOME

BE AMAZING

OR

GO HOME

SEVEN CUSTOMER SERVICE HABITS
THAT CREATE CONFIDENCE WITH EVERYONE

SHEP HYKEN

NEW YORK TIMES AND *WALL STREET JOURNAL* BESTSELLING AUTHOR

Published and Distributed by
SOUND WISDOM
PO Box 310
Shippensburg, PA 17257-0310
717-530-2122
info@soundwisdom.com
www.soundwisdom.com

Be Amazing or Go Home
Seven Customer Service Habits that Create Confidence with Everyone
Shep Hyken
1. Customer Service. 2. Consumer satisfaction. 3. Employee empowerment. 4. Corporate culture. 5. Success in business. I. Title.

ISBN 13 TP: 978-1-64095-149-5
ISBN 13 eBook: 978-1-64095-150-1

Previously published under ISBN 978-0-9637820-7-6
For Worldwide Distribution, Printed in the U.S.A.
1 2 3 4 5 6 / 22 21 20 19

BOOKS BY SHEP HYKEN

Moments of Magic: Be a Star with Your

Customer and Keep Them Forever

The Loyal Customer: A Lesson from a Cad Driver

Only the Best on Success (coauthor)

Only the Best on Customer Service (coauthor)

Only the Best on Leadership (coauthor)

The Winning Spirit (coauthor)

Inspiring Others to Win (coauthor)

The Cult of the Customer: Create an Amazing Experience That

Turns Satisfied Customers into Customer Evangelists

The Amazement Revolution: Seven Customer Service Strategies to

Create an Amazing Customer (and Employee) Experience

Amaze Every Customer Every Time: 52 Tools for Delivering the Most

Amazing Customer Service on the Planet

Be Amazing or Go Home: Seven Customer Service

Habits That Create Confidence with Everyone

The Convenience Revolution: How to Deliver a Customer Service

Experience that Disrupts the Competition and Creates Fierce Loyalty

CONTENTS

A special gift for you!

As a special thank you, be sure to visit
www.BeAmazingOrGoHome.com
for your free gift!

(And you'll be happy you did!)

And don't forget to follow me:

ShepHykenSpeaker   ShepHyken   @hyken   ShepHyken

PROLOGUE

SHOW GRATITUDE—THE FOUNDATION OF AMAZEMENT

Amazing people appreciate what they have and express appreciation to others.

GRATITUDE IS A VITALLY important habit. Amazing people appreciate everything they have, both the good and the bad. Why the bad? Because they know they can learn from it, which makes them even better.

Amazing people make others feel appreciated. They know the power of an authentic "Thank you." They know how recognizing and expressing appreciation makes others feel good.

That is why, before we go further, I want to express gratitude to you, the reader. Thank you! This book is for you. It is my belief that if you can find even one usable idea in a book, the investment you made in it—both the dollars and the time—will have paid off. So I hope you find an idea in the book that you can use—and then even more. Because if one idea is big, then more than one idea is...Amazing!

Look at that. Our first lesson, and the book hasn't even "officially" started yet.

- Saying "Thank you," and meaning it, makes others feel appreciated, special, and recognized.

- Don't assume people know you're grateful for what they do. Make *sure* they know.

- Be grateful for both the opportunities and the setbacks that come your way. You can learn from both.

ARE YOU AMAZING?

People do business with people, not organizations—and they do more business, more often, with AMAZING people.

THAT'S THE CORE PRINCIPLE supporting everything you will read in these pages. Now that I've shared that vitally important idea with you, I'd like to continue by sharing with you exactly how I decided to write this book so you'll know why you should continue to read it. What I'm about to share with you is something that really happened, not all that long ago. I've changed the names and some of the details in order to, as the saying goes, "protect the innocent."

Once upon a time, Heidi worked for my company, Shepard Presentations. When Heidi first started with us, about a year earlier, she was what we call *Amazing*— meaning she consistently made a point of delivering *above-average* service to both internal customers, the people she worked with, and external customers, the clients with whom we do business. We have a mantra at our company: "Always Be Amazing!" Amazing people inspire confidence in others. Heidi, like everyone else in our organization, had a lot of fun living up to that saying. In fact, the whole reason I hired her was that she agreed, with enthusiasm, to make that saying the central element of her job description.

Heidi consistently delivered above-average service to everyone who came in contact with her. I wasn't the only one who thought Heidi was Amazing. We all thought so, we all told her so, and all of our customers also agreed!

At this point, for more than a year, Heidi had consistently come to work on time, if not a little early. Now, Heidi knew that at Shepard Presentations, getting to work at 8:00 a.m. wasn't really showing up on time. While our office is officially open for business at 8:00 a.m., showing up on time means you're *ready to go* when we open. And by the way, that's part of how we define an Amazing experience for one another internally at Shepard Presentations: showing up *on time*. That's one of the values that shape our working culture. We'll be talking a lot about working culture in the pages that follow.

Heidi worked hard. She hit deadlines. She shared great ideas with the team. She was helping to redefine how we did business. Our clients loved her. We loved her. And she loved us. Then one day, something changed.

One day, I noticed Heidi had come in late, without so much as a word of explanation. She was not that late, just a few minutes. But the late arrival was definitely out of character for her—and inconsistent with the Amazement culture that is the foundation of our organization. I also noticed that morning that Heidi wasn't smiling, which seemed unusual. Something was wrong.

I sat down next to Heidi in her work area, and I asked her if everything was OK. She assured me that she felt fine. Still, I could tell the fire that had been in her eyes, the enthusiasm for Amazement that she had exhibited for more than a year, was not there. There was a problem. As the day moved forward, it seemed like Heidi was just going through the motions.

My philosophy is that bad days last only twenty-four hours. I hoped that by the next day, everything would return to normal with Heidi. Unfortunately, that was not the case. Heidi started arriving late to work every day, something I couldn't even have imagined before. She also wasn't smiling very much. The pattern continued for more than a week. It was time for us to have a one-on-one talk.

Privately, I went over my concerns, which weren't just about the tardiness. Yes, I did want to talk about when Heidi was showing up for work, and as I mentioned, being on time might mean showing up just a little early. But I also wanted to land the important point that when you do show up right on time, you also need to show up *ready to go*—because if you're not mentally present, you're really not there. Lately, I'd had the sense that Heidi wasn't really there, even after she'd shown up.

While everyone is going to have a bad day every once in a while, if you find you're having a bad week or a bad month, it affects your long-term performance and can even impact the team's performance and morale. A long-term slump is something that needs to be discussed, because it affects the *confidence* that customers and coworkers have in you.

Heidi and I had a long one-on-one talk about being Amazing. I reminded her, gently but firmly, that being Amazing was one of the most important parts of her job description, that it was part of the culture of our organization, and that it was what everyone else in the office had committed to, including but not limited to the goal of being on time or early for work each morning. Heidi took it all in, nodded optimistically, and said she understood and would make sure she got back into Amazing mode, starting immediately.

Good news! The next day, she showed up on time. Bad news! A week later, she was late again. And again the next day. Even more ominously, her usual excellent work was now slipping further. She seemed tense, unfocused, and even a little frantic when challenges came up. Things were getting worse, not better. After a few more days of this, I realized it was time for us to have our second private talk.

Heidi had a lot of great reasons for being late, and she shared them with me in detail as the meeting began.

She wanted me to know, first and foremost, that the lateness problem wasn't really her fault. She blamed it on the traffic. This was totally out of character for Heidi. She had always accepted responsibility for all of her actions and had been one of the most accountable people I'd ever met. Normally, she would be talking about what she could do to resolve the problem, talking about what she was personally responsible for. But now, she was just making excuses.

Calmly, I told Heidi that this meeting really wasn't about whether she had a great *reason* for being consistently late. It was about whether she was still willing to inspire Amazement in others—to deliver above-average service to our customers and to her colleagues.

I reminded her that when she accepted a job with my company, she understood exactly what Amazement was and that she had agreed, in a one-on-one meeting like the one we were having now, to live by Amazement as the "compass point" of our working culture—just as everyone else had agreed to do, including me.

Then I reminded her of something else that was a central principle at Shepard Presentations: We hire only Amazing people...and we strive to make every single one of our relationships—with customers and with everyone else—Amazing.

Heidi nodded solemnly as I made each of these points, and she didn't make any attempt to challenge anything I was saying. I told her I had three questions to ask her.

The first was about whether I was right in assuming that something big had changed in her life that affected how she was performing. The answer to that question, as it turned out, was "Yes." It wasn't anything I could have helped her to deal with, but it was something major that had changed in her world.

I then asked her whether she felt her performance during the past month had been Amazing or anything close to it. She agreed that it wasn't, and she even volunteered that it was unlikely to *become* Amazing again anytime soon.

Finally, I asked her whether she thought she would be happier somewhere else. This really wasn't meant as any kind of threat. I want people working at Shepard Presentations to be happy. If they aren't, I want to help them, if possible, find another job elsewhere.

"Here's the thing, Heidi," I said. "You know we hire only Amazing people here, and you just told me that you're not hitting that standard. I think we've reached the point where you have one of two choices:

"You can be Amazing...or go home."

She laughed a little at that and said it was a pretty good line. She told me that I ought to write it down so I didn't forget it. She even said, "That would be a good title for a book." (I did write it down, and I kept writing on that theme for weeks to come. You're holding the result in your hands.)

Heidi made her decision. She chose to *go home*. It was the right decision. I'm happy to report that Heidi voluntarily found employment elsewhere and is doing well there. We're still on very good terms. I see her regularly. There's no bitterness. There's no resentment. She just hit an Amazement barrier, and she needed a change to get over it. We decided, together, during that meeting that she was no longer a good fit. I'm very grateful to her for all the contributions she made while she was with us. And I'm just as grateful to her for realizing that it really was time for her to make a choice.

In the end, the choice Heidi had to make is the same choice we all face in our professional lives each and every day. We can be Amazing. We can inspire confidence. Or we can go home.

Amazement...it's the standard I see demonstrated by world-class people and organizations.

I truly believe that our organizations can be Amazing day in and day out, week in and week out, month in and month out. I also believe that when our customers, colleagues, and others we connect with come to count on us to be Amazing, we can build extraordinary relationships that make a difference.

I wrote this book because I believe that anyone, in any enterprise, is capable of being Amazing. It really is a matter of personal commitment.

Once you make a powerful personal commitment to work with, be around, and build Amazing rela-

tionships, a new personal and professional standard emerges for creating confidence within those relationships: BE AMAZING...OR GO HOME!

THE ANATOMY OF AMAZEMENT

What is Amazement? If you don't know, you should find out...before your competition does.

AMAZING (ADJ): causing great surprise or wonder: causing amazement

That's how the *Merriam-Webster Dictionary* defines the word *amazing*. To convey what *I* mean by Amazing, with a capital *A*, I need to stop for a moment and share several other important phrases with you. These phrases have been a part of every book that I've written. If you're familiar with my work, you'll recognize these concepts, and the brief explanations that follow will serve as a short refresher course. If this is the first time you've encountered these ideas, consider what follows as foundation points for the principles we'll be covering together here.

Moment of Truth is a term that was coined by Jan Carlzon, the former president of Scandinavian Airlines. Carlzon defined the Moment of Truth in business as *any time the customer comes into contact with any aspect of a business, however remote, and has an opportunity to form an impression.* According to Carlzon, Moments of Truth can be good or bad. I believe there is a third possibility, and that's average. Below are the three terms that I use to describe these three different Moments of Truth.

A *Moment of Misery* is a negative interaction. You've certainly experienced at least one of these yourself—it's a problem that leads to a complaint. For instance: A call to a company's customer service line that results in an unacceptably long wait, possibly accompanied by bad "hold music," just to complain about a problem such as a shipping error. That definitely counts as a Moment of Misery. So does an e-mail about a vital issue sent to a colleague who ignores it for two days, even though you asked in the subject line, politely and tactfully, for a quick response. These are examples of Moments of Misery, moments and interactions that threaten the confidence and quality of the relationship. They come in any number of situations and are just as likely to involve a text or an e-mail as they are a face-to-face or voice-to-voice conversation.

A *Moment of Mediocrity* is just what it sounds like— an average or mediocre service experience. It doesn't stand out. It's not positive. It's not negative. It could be considered only satisfactory or average. It's just there.

Someone does the job but does only the bare minimum necessary to support the relationship. If you've ever done business with someone who does only what is absolutely essential, perhaps with an apathetic attitude or without showing any genuine interest toward you as a person, someone who was just going through the motions, then you've experienced a Moment of Mediocrity.

A ***Moment of Magic*** is a *positive* interaction or touch point with a customer or colleague. Of course, these too come in many different forms—person-to-person, voice-to-voice, or even digitally. Please don't get hung up on the word *magic*. Magic doesn't mean "WOW" or "blow me away with incredible, over-the-top service," although it could. Typically, a Moment of Magic is simply an *above-average experience*. Sometimes it's a little bit better than average or satisfactory. Sometimes it can be that "WOW" moment or an instance of someone truly going the extra mile. Most of the time, however, a Moment of Magic is simply the positive, above-average way a company or individual handles business. Once in a while, these moments arise out of Moments of Misery. If there is a complaint or a problem that is resolved properly, you can effectively turn *misery* into *magic*. This is often where the over-the-top, above-and-beyond experiences happen: from problems or complaints. They are gifts, in a sense, because the customer is handing you the opportunity to fix a problem and show how good you are. If that opportunity comes your way, seize it.

Every Moment of Truth, even if it is a Moment of Misery, is an opportunity to create a Moment of Magic.

Amazement is now pretty easy for us to define in detail. **Amazement is a predictable and consistent above-average experience. It's a *sequence* of Moments of Magic *consistent* enough to inspire *confidence* in our customers, our colleagues, and just about everyone else we encounter.**

FROM MISERY TO AMAZEMENT

Amazement in action is something you never forget.

NOT LONG AGO, I was staying at a Ritz-Carlton Hotel to speak at a client's event. I love it when my clients stay at Amazing hotels. The Ritz-Carlton chain is such an Amazing institution; it has built Amazement into the very fabric of its organization.

Just after I checked in, I went to my room, and I noticed something unusual: a couple of dirty towels the last guest had left behind that housekeeping had somehow missed. They lay crumpled in the corner of my bathroom. I thought to myself, *Interesting. That's not what usually happens here.* (Yes, that counts as a Moment of Misery.)

Early that evening, there was a knock at the door. It

was a member of the housekeeping staff who was there to do the turndown service, which included closing curtains, preparing the bed (as in taking off all the fancy pillows and bedspread), and freshening up the room. As she came in, I smiled and said, "Hi." Then I mentioned, "There are some dirty towels in here from the previous guest. They're in the corner in the bathroom."

The housekeeper, Andrea, was appalled, even a little embarrassed. She apologized immediately, assumed full responsibility for the situation, and said she would take care of cleaning up the used towels and getting fresh ones.

So far, so good! A modest Moment of Magic. The accountability she showed was definitely above average.

Now, I happen to know that the Ritz-Carlton gives all of its staff members (including housekeepers) the ability to spend up to $2,000, on their own authority, to fix a customer problem. Knowing this led me to wonder what might happen next. Truth be told, I didn't expect any kind of cash-reward treatment for something as minor as a dirty towel. Yet, I was curious about what the response might be.

Andrea finished taking care of the room and apologized again for the dirty towels before she left. I eventually headed out to dinner. When I came back a few hours later, I found there was a little note card on the bed pillow, and next to it was a small golden box. I shook my head. What did the note say, and what was in the box?

I opened the envelope and read a personal, handwritten note of apology from Andrea for those dirty towels. When I opened the golden box, I saw that it contained a delicious-looking chocolate truffle, which by the way, tasted even better than it looked.

Talk about a Moment of Magic! What I saw on that pillow was something I will never forget. I've shared the story with hundreds of people, and now I've shared it with you. How much do you think it cost? Maybe a dollar? Obviously, nothing close to the $2,000 the Ritz-Carlton housekeepers are authorized to spend to take care of a guest who has experienced a problem. Yet, what she spent—the cost of a piece of chocolate and the signed note—was absolutely appropriate. It was Amazement in action.

That experience tells you something about the good people the hotel hires, the great training those people receive, and the strong culture of Amazement that's earned the Ritz-Carlton hotel chain its stellar reputation.

THE SEVEN AMAZEMENT HABITS

When you make Amazement your consistent way of doing business, people come to count on you and want to be in your circle.

WHY HAVE I TOLD you these two stories—of Heidi, who worked for me, and Andrea, the housekeeper who worked for the Ritz-Carlton? Because the stories are opposites that, taken together, provide a clear picture of both the good and bad habits that affect the pursuit of Amazement.

Amazing people have (at least) seven specific, predictable habits. When we practice these habits consistently, day in and day out, other people come to count on us and want to be in our circle. The people could be customers or colleagues or even those with whom we have personal relationships. These are the

habits that instill confidence. They help us succeed, get promoted, build business, earn referrals, and more. Sometimes they just make others want to be around us.

The seven Amazement Habits are as follows. As you read through them, notice how the stories about Andrea, the housekeeper at the Ritz-Carlton, and Heidi, my employee at Shepard Presentations, illustrate both the positive and negative sides of how the habits operate—or don't.

Habit No. 1: Amazing People Show Up Ready to Amaze. Andrea, the housekeeper, was ready and able to Amaze when the opportunity presented itself. Heidi had fallen out of the habit.

Habit No. 2: Amazing People Are Proactive. Nothing in the "rule book" told Andrea how to respond to the specific situation she faced, but she still knew what to do. Heidi had been in the habit of acting proactively but had allowed herself to slip.

Habit No. 3: Amazing People Want Feedback. Andrea listened to my problem with undivided attention. Heidi, on the other hand, had reached a point where she was resistant to feedback.

Habit No. 4: Amazing People Take Personal Responsibility. Andrea hadn't left the dirty towels in the bathroom—someone on an earlier shift had. But she took on full accountability for resolving the problem as though she *had* left them. Heidi made excuses about why she was late day after day. In her view, the problem wasn't her fault.

Habit No. 5: Amazing People Are Authentic. Andrea meant every word that came out of her mouth. How do I know? She said she would fix the problem, and she did. Heidi said she would show up on time, and she didn't— making a promise that she didn't keep.

Habit No. 6: Amazing People Turn Misery into Magic. Andrea took something bad and fixed it—actually, she made it better. Heidi took a bad experience and repeated it.

Habit No. 7: Amazing People Focus on Excellence. Andrea was fully invested in making sure I had a great stay. She was totally committed to creating an above-average experience for me. Heidi's commitment to our company and her coworkers, by her own admission, had slipped over time. The excellence of the relationship, and the overall experience, was no longer a major priority for her. She was just getting through the day.

I believe people and organizations can and should adopt these seven Amazement Habits—and make Amazement a way of life—in order to create deeper confidence in those with whom they interact. If you agree—if you're not ready to go home but would rather choose to be Amazing—then please keep reading.

THE FIRST HABIT:

AMAZING PEOPLE SHOW UP READY TO AMAZE

SHOW UP READY TO AMAZE

Amazement is all about showing up at the top of your game.

I STARTED MY FIRST business when I was twelve years old. You could say that I was the product and that my job was to create Amazement.

The business was performing magic shows at birthday parties. My very first show was in front of twenty boisterous six-year-olds, probably the most terrifying audience I've ever faced. I was pretty nervous before I stepped in front of that group of screaming kids, yet somehow, the show went on.

It went well—better than I had expected. The kids were happy. The parents were happy. In fact, the birthday boy's parents started recommending me to their friends.

Before I knew it, I was performing as many as ten magic shows each week. My little business began to grow.

Once they realized I was an entrepreneur, my parents sat me down from time to time to give me advice about my new venture. I didn't realize it back then, but they were teaching me some of the basics of good customer service.

Case in point: I had thought I could save myself some time—and maximize my income potential—by walking into the home where I was booked to perform just a few minutes before I was supposed to go on. For me—the twelve-year-old entrepreneur—being "on time" meant I had to show up five minutes early to be set up and ready to perform at the agreed-upon time. Why not cut it close? After all, the more shows I could do on a Saturday afternoon, the more money I could earn. And it took almost no time at all to set up my props. All the parents had to do was point to the room where they wanted me to perform, and I was ready to go in less than a minute.

My dad, however, had a different take on this issue. He said, "Shep, let's say your show is supposed to start at one o'clock. When do you think the parents are going to start looking at their watches and wondering, 'What time is the magician going to show up?'"

"Hmm," I said, pretending I would have thought this through on my own if I'd been given the time. "Probably about fifteen minutes or so before show time."

"Exactly," he said, smiling.

My dad told me in no uncertain terms that from that

point forward, if I didn't arrive at least fifteen minutes before the show was supposed to start, I would be late. So I made it my practice to be at least twenty minutes early for a booking. And I found out that eliminating one show on a Saturday and giving my customers a little more time actually meant doing *more* business long term.

- **Amazement is all about creating confidence.** If something you're doing makes the other person less confident about the relationship, then you need to change what you're doing. Otherwise, you risk losing future business and referrals.

- **Woody Allen was only partially right.** In 1989, Allen told the *New York Times* language columnist William Safire[1] that he, Allen, had coined the maxim, "Eighty percent of success is showing up." Today, I'd amend Mr. Allen's rule to read, "Eighty percent of success is showing up...in a manner that's Amazing." For example, it's one thing to show up. It's another to show up on time—maybe even early.

- **Make it a habit to show up at the top of your game.** Don't just show up. Show up ready to Amaze everyone, every time.

---

1   http://quoteinvestigator.com/2013/06/10/showing-up/

WORK ON LOMBARDI TIME

Set a higher standard. Never be late. People who count on you shouldn't have to wait to get a great experience.

THE BIG LIFE LESSON I just shared with you, the lesson about showing up ready to Amaze, came to me from my dad when I was a kid. Years later, I learned that Vince Lombardi, the Hall of Fame football coach who won multiple National Football League (NFL) championships with the Green Bay Packers (including the first two Super Bowls) had a lot in common with my father. Lombardi had a strikingly similar definition of the phrase "on time." He used to tell his players to show up for practice at least fifteen minutes early. Any later than that, and they would be considered tardy—and treated accordingly.

In other words, Lombardi believed that being *technically* on time wasn't good enough for a championship team, and that was the only kind of team he was interested in working with. His insistence on punctuality was part of his legendary passion for excellence.

This was just one of the ways that Lombardi made a habit of holding himself and others to a higher standard than most people in the NFL—indeed, in all professional sports—were used to. One of his favorite sayings was, "Perfection is not attainable. But if we chase perfection, we can catch excellence." I love that.

Lombardi's insistence on being fifteen minutes early to every team event was part of that endless quest for perfection. It was one of the nonnegotiable requirements of being a part of the Packers, and guess what? Everyone embraced it. Showing up fifteen minutes before the scheduled start time became part of the team culture, part of how the Green Bay Packers did business.

Around the locker room and on the practice field, the Packers built an obsession for being in the right place at least a quarter of an hour before they were supposed to, and the habit eventually became known as "Lombardi Time."

A few years back, the city of Green Bay, Wisconsin, paid Lombardi a remarkable tribute. On July 20, 2012, the big clock at Lambeau Field—the legendary venue where the Packers still play and where Lombardi coached his team to a dynasty—was set fifteen minutes ahead of the actual time. That clock is *always* on Lombardi Time.

Most people who pass the clock never notice this. Only a few wonder why the clock always runs ahead of schedule. Here's the answer: The huge clock that looks out on Lombardi Avenue reminds everyone of the extraordinary personal and organizational discipline that was Coach Lombardi's hallmark. *He lived this standard.* That's why he was able to get other people to live it. He followed it himself.

Some people hear me talk about this and assume I'm suggesting everyone should run their team exactly the way Lombardi ran his. They assume I'm telling leaders to demand that everyone show up for meetings a quarter of an hour before the meetings are scheduled to start. Actually, that's *not* what I'm saying. Instead, I'm suggesting a much more powerful goal. Ask yourself:

How can you best adapt the spirit of Lombardi Time into your world?

Before you try to answer that, let me share a true story that illustrates what I mean. Not long ago, I discussed all of this with one of my colleagues, Buddy Rice. Buddy is one of our Amazing customer service trainers at Shepard Presentations. He came to us from the corporate world, having worked for Delta Airlines. For a long time, he was in charge of the Delta Sky Clubs (formerly Crown Rooms) around the world. When Buddy heard me talking about the importance of showing up *ready to Amaze*, he shared a recent experience.

As part of his regular oversight of the Delta clubs, Buddy would show up right around opening time, just like a passenger on an early morning flight would. One of the clubs he was responsible for opened at 4:30 a.m. daily. He showed up at this club a few minutes before 4:30 a.m., along with several passengers who were hoping to enjoy some coffee while waiting for their flights. (Notice that Buddy was himself on the job early, which I would say counts as living up to the Lombardi standard.)

At exactly 4:30 a.m., the employee opening the club showed up, unlocked the door, and let everyone in. The problem was, she still had to turn on the computer and get ready to check all the members in. And she hadn't even started brewing the coffee.

Yes, she apologized for making everyone wait. But that's not the point. Technically, the club was open at 4:30 a.m. In terms of the customer experience, though, it really didn't start *feeling* like it was open until about 4:45 a.m. And what the experience *feels* like to the other person is what counts.

Long story short: It wasn't an Amazing opening.

Buddy had a heart-to-heart conversation with that employee. He reminded her that the club was supposed to *open* at 4:30 a.m., which meant she needed to be *ready to welcome* the members at 4:30 a.m., not just open the doors. His suggestion was that she make a point of being there at least fifteen minutes early to get the computers turned on and the coffee brewing.

From that point on, she was never "late" again.

I don't know what "Lombardi Time" is when translated into practical terms for your organization. It might be ten minutes ahead of a scheduled commitment. It might be fifteen. It might be something else entirely. But I do know this: **If you're keeping people who trust you waiting or making them wonder when you will show up, you're not Amazing them.** You're undermining their confidence in the relationship. Amazement is always defined by the other person, not by us. We can only do our best and hope that they agree we have met their expectations. We can try to be Amazing, but other people tell us if we succeeded. It's harder to get that response if you start the relationship by making somebody wait.

- **Act like a member of a championship team.** Set a nonnegotiable standard that says, "We show up ready to Amaze." Then honor it yourself. No one else will honor the standard if you don't.

- **People who count on us shouldn't have to wait to get a great experience.** This applies to everyone, but it's a particularly important standard for interactions with customers. Ask yourself: What happens when you keep a customer waiting? What conclusions does the customer draw about you and your organization?

- **Send others the silent message, "I respect your time."** When you show up on time, that's what's expected. Showing up late is simply disrespectful. What message do you send to a friend or work colleague when you agree to meet for lunch at noon, and you show up five or ten minutes late? Whose time are you saying is more important?

REMEMBER: YOU'RE ALWAYS ON STAGE

When it comes to Amazement, make a habit of aiming high. People are watching.

STAGE AND SCREEN ACTOR Richard Burton supposedly summed up the key to his success with the following words: "I want to be so good tonight that I cheat the audience that was here the night before."

When I share that quote with audiences, some of them get a confused look on their faces. (By the way, if you're one of the people thinking, *Who is Richard Burton?*, I'll get to that in a second.)

Like many other aspects of Burton's life, this sentence about being so good you make the previous night's audience feel they missed out on something special is rich in both plausibility and legend. In fact, it may be more legend than truth, but my view is that if Burton didn't say these words, he should have. Regardless of who uttered these words first, they sum up Burton's extraordinary career perfectly, and that's why I'm sharing his story with you here.

Burton was an extraordinary actor who was totally committed to his craft, committed to it as few actors of any generation have been. Widely respected among his peers for his perfectionism and professionalism, Burton suffered through many ups and downs because of personal problems, but he never compromised a performance or took an audience for granted. His superb work in classical theater, television, and Hollywood blockbusters led to countless accolades, including seven Academy Award nominations and a Tony Award for Best Actor. But that's not why I want you to remember this remarkable quote.

I want you to remember it because it works. The idea is to be so good, or at least try to be so good, that you set a brand-new standard every time you step onto the stage. And when you stop to think about it, you realize that we are *all* performers for some kind of audience. As William Shakespeare said in *As You Like It*, Act II, Scene VII: "All the world's a stage; and all the men and women merely players." Remembering this is a powerful and reliable foundation for showing up ready to Amaze.

The very best professionals, the ones we want to be around and stay around, know there is no such thing as "downtime." They know that when it comes to workplace relationships, they really are always on stage—and they really do have to aim to be better, each and every time they step onto that stage. That's a high standard, but it's one that truly Amazing people are willing to take on. I call it the Burton Standard.

The Burton Standard builds great reputations—and great brands.

Whenever you are in front of a customer or a work colleague, for any reason and anywhere, assume you are "on stage." Make sure it's a great performance. Your brand—both personal and organizational—depends on that commitment. You may not always hit the goal of giving a greater performance each time, but you can always aim for it. Everything about what we do is a performance: the way we look, the clothes we wear, our body language, the way we talk, the words we choose, and our tone of voice. Everything.

By the same token, *forgetting* that we are always on stage is what *damages* our reputation and our personal brand. Remember: Branding is what we *tell* people we want them to think about us. We try to assign a message. For instance, we may want customers and colleagues to conclude that we are friendly, that we are nice, that we care, that we always follow through—whatever it is. But people aren't going to trust that until they experience it for themselves. Inevitably, the question becomes: *Does the perception that we want the person to have align with the actual experience we deliver?*

And the answer is, *the customer gets to choose*, based on the quality of our performance at any given moment.

We don't choose. We only get to choose how we want people to feel. Our "audiences" get to choose how they actually feel, and whether it matched up with what we promised. The Burton Standard helps us to remember this.

We can set an expectation in the other person's mind. But we need to remember, as Richard Burton always did, that our customers are an audience. *They* get to say whether or not we meet expectations, whether to applaud or boo. It's like that not only with customers but also with everyone in our world. We set the expectations, and it's up to the other person to decide whether or not we meet them.

The Burton Standard reminds us, powerfully, that once is not enough, and that "good enough" is never really good enough.

Let's say I'm a customer. I like what happens the first time—you give me what you promised. Great! But until I experience it again, and maybe again and again, I'm not going to trust that this is the way it's always going to happen.

The Burton Standard reminds us that we should aspire not to just meet the minimum standard—that's a Moment of Mediocrity, after all—but to raise the bar and keep it high.

If we aim low, if we aim to meet the minimum standard, we're like everyone else. We won't have a competitive edge. We won't build up any trust in the quality of the experience. To do that, we should aspire to improve the quality of our own performance, every day. That's what

Richard Burton did—and he won the Tony Award for Best Actor on Broadway for his efforts.

- **Live by the Burton Standard.** Commit to being better today than yesterday. Adopt it as your professional aspiration. Whenever you interact with a customer or a colleague, aim to be so good that you raise the bar—no matter how good you were last time.

- **You can't be great one day and just OK the next.** Inconsistency lets down the "audience" and hurts your brand.

- **You may not always hit the mark of giving a better performance,** but you can always aim for that. If you aim higher each time, the quality of the experience you actually deliver will improve.

LOOK BEYOND THE CLOCK

Act like you're on the clock...even when you're not.

RECENTLY, I WENT TO the movie theater with my kids. We were there for the early afternoon show, and so were a few other customers. My kids and I were at the front of the line. It wasn't moving. While waiting inside the cinema complex to buy our tickets, we watched as the two employees behind the counter chatted amiably with each other. They didn't even bother to glance our way. They were completely ignoring us.

It was obvious we were waiting to purchase tickets, and we were standing only a few feet away from these employees. It felt as though they thought we didn't exist. As we stood there watching, waiting for one of the two young ladies to acknowledge our presence, one of them picked up her cell phone to make a personal call.

I couldn't believe it. By this point, we had been standing there looking at them for what must have been five minutes. When I decided to break the silence by stepping forward and asking to buy a ticket, the employee who wasn't chatting away on her phone informed me that the box office wasn't going to be open for another four minutes. (This information, by the way, wasn't posted anywhere that I could see.)

Without so much as an "Excuse me," the employee went right back to ignoring us, and her companion kept on with her cell phone conversation.

I shook my head in astonishment and asked, "I'm sorry, but if the cinema is closed, how come the doors are unlocked?"

She shrugged and said, "I don't know." Then she walked away.

These two employees continued to ignore us—and everyone else who was in line. They didn't want to speak to us again until the moment they were officially on the clock.

Two of the other customers became annoyed with this treatment and left. We didn't, because we really wanted to see the film. But I can tell you that our experience at the cinema did not start out well that day.

These employees were in uniform and were standing right in front of their paying customers. We had no way of knowing when we could expect to buy a ticket. The two young ladies behind the counter may not have technically been on duty, but they were still representing the theater. The *least* they could have done was apologize for the delay and tell us they would be with us in just a few minutes. What kind of an impression do you think they were making for the theater?

For me, this was like what might happen if you were cut off by a truck on the highway, and then you recognized the company name painted on the side of the truck. You would not only be mad at the driver; you would be mad at the whole company. I don't blame just the two ladies selling tickets; I also blame the theater and the management for what happened. This kind of thing is not just a failure of basic common sense; it's a failure of training.

The lesson here goes to the fundamentals of service. The employees of that movie theater blew the basic concept: Any contact that a customer has with a company, or any employee of that company, is an opportunity to create an impression—good, bad, or mediocre. Everyone working with any company or organization must recognize this. When it comes to relationships with customers—or work colleagues, for that matter—hiding behind the clock and pretending someone doesn't exist is a great way to launch a Moment of Misery. Simply put, don't do it!

- **Don't have a clock-in, clock-out mentality.** The other person doesn't care what your time sheet says. If you are representing your organization, assume you are always "on the clock."

- **Never allow people who are counting on you to feel ignored.** Take responsibility for every exchange. Engage. Interact. If there's a difficult situation, explain what's happening.

- **When faced with a challenge, look at the relationship first.** Connect with the other person as a human being, no matter what time it is. Don't try to pretend he or she begins to exist only once you are "on the clock."

ENTER THE ANTI-NO ZONE

Imagine a world where the word no isn't the first option.

WHAT IS AN ANTI-NO Zone? Exactly what it sounds like. This breakthrough idea is all about creating a space where you're not automatically saying no to someone who's counting on you.

That doesn't mean you have to always say yes. There will be plenty of times you will have to find a creative way to deal with someone's request. Maybe the request isn't something you or your organization does. Maybe it's an item that is out of stock. Maybe you simply can't fulfill what the other person is asking for. Maybe the request is illegal. Regardless of the reason you can't do exactly what the person wants, it is the *spirit* of Anti-No that Amazing people focus on. They try to come up with a reasonable yes alternative or solution that makes the other person happy.

A friend of mine booked a room at a nice little bed and breakfast. He did this six weeks ahead of time, using an online booking service to make the reservation. His credit card was charged for the deposit. He received an online confirmation that everything was in order. When the morning of the day of his stay came around, he phoned the bed and breakfast before he left home, hoping to make sure, voice to voice, that the reservation was all set up. For some reason, the bed and breakfast people weren't answering the phone, so he left a message that said, basically, "Hi. I booked a room six weeks ago. The e-mail confirmation says I'm all set. Here's my phone number. Please call me if there's any problem." (Of course, the confirmation e-mail he'd received was more than enough to establish all that, but my friend believes in double-checking these kinds of things.)

He didn't receive a call back from the bed and breakfast, which he took to mean that there was no problem with the reservation. My friend was looking forward to a nice stay.

However, when he showed up with his luggage at the front door of the bed and breakfast, it turned out that there *was* a problem. Although my friend wanted to check in immediately, he couldn't. The booking service had double-booked the room. There were now absolutely no more rooms left. My friend was disappointed, and he said so.

But then look at what happened. The owner of the bed and breakfast didn't just dump the problem back in my friend's lap and say, "Not our fault—the online booking service you used made a mistake," even though that was technically true. Instead, she said, "Listen, I'm really sorry. There's been a technical problem here, and your room was double-booked. I know this isn't what you had in mind. Let me make a suggestion. There's a little restaurant across the street. Why don't you go in there and grab some lunch? Keep the receipt. We'll reimburse you for that. Come back in forty-five minutes or an hour, and I'll have this worked out for you."

She was as good as her word. When my friend got back from lunch, she had booked him a room at the same price at a competing bed and breakfast that was just two blocks away. That's what an Anti-No Zone looks like. She *could* have said something like, "No, we can't do anything to help you because it's not our fault/not our policy/not our problem," but she chose not to.

It's easy to tell Anti-No Zones from everywhere else. When you're in an Anti-No Zone, you know that people are open to at least a conversation with you about what should happen next. An Anti-No Zone welcomes creative thinking about how to make the best outcome happen for both parties. Win-win outcomes are common. Customers (and others) *love* to get evidence that they've landed in a zone like this, and the earlier they get that evidence, the better.

Most of us are used to landing in a No Zone—that cold, gray space where the default answer is always no, the dialogues are short, the outcomes are all predictable no matter what anyone says, and the winners and losers are all sorted out well ahead of time.

A while back, I was at a restaurant, and I asked the server to replace the string beans that came with the entrée I ordered with a different vegetable—broccoli, which was also on the menu. You know what he said? "No. The vegetables are already preportioned and precooked. No substitutions." Can you guess which zone I was in? Can you guess how I felt about that meal I was paying a premium price for? (And the vegetables weren't even fresh.)

A few days later, I found myself at another restaurant, facing almost the same situation. The vegetables that came with the meal were a medley of squash, cauliflower, and broccoli. I asked if I could have just broccoli. You know what the server said? "Yes. We do everything we can to accommodate all our guests' special requests." They took the other restaurant's Moment of Misery and created a Moment of Magic.

Notice that the Anti-No Zone isn't about fixing a problem. It's about engaging in a dialogue with the customer without saying no. Are you going to be able to say yes every single time? Maybe not, but it's nice to make an effort. One thing's for sure: You wouldn't bark out the words *No substitutions!* to your best friend or your best customer.

More people and teams should set up an Anti-No Zone.

I'm certainly not saying that we need to capitulate to every request, no matter how unreasonable. But the culture of the enterprise should incline toward looking creatively for a way to say yes and create an early win-win outcome. That should be our first effort.

Can't you visualize the logo—a big red circle with the word *NO* in the middle and a red line through it? Or how about a sign that says, "You are entering the ANTI-NO ZONE"?

- **Could an Anti-No Zone work for your business?** Consider an initiative that instructs employees to avoid knee-jerk "No" answers to customer requests. There is always a better response than that.

- **Empower employees to say yes, and give them clear guidelines about when and how to do so.** Maybe it is impossible to always say yes. Even so, showing up ready to Amaze means understanding and embracing the philosophy of avoiding the word *no* and engaging in a real dialogue with the other person.

- **Reward team members who find appropriate alternatives to "No."** Help them look for new ways to deliver great service, create confidence, de-escalate when conversations get tense, avoid Moments of Misery, and create Moments of Magic.

KEY TAKEAWAYS FOR THE FIRST HABIT:
AMAZING PEOPLE SHOW UP READY TO AMAZE

- Make it a habit to show up at the top of your game. Send others the silent message, "I respect your time." Being late sends the message, "I'm more important than you."

- Set a higher standard. That may mean showing up a little early.

- Remember: You're always on stage.

- Don't have a clock-in, clock-out mentality. Let people who count on you know that you're there for them, regardless of what time it is.

- Empower other people to say yes, and give them clear guidelines about when to do so. Reward them when they do.

THE SECOND HABIT:

AMAZING PEOPLE ARE PROACTIVE

BE PROACTIVE

Don't wait for things to happen. Make them happen.

THE SECOND HABIT THAT all truly Amazing people and teams share is *being proactive*. This means taking the initiative to anticipate what needs to be done in order to keep Moments of Misery from happening in the first place.

Very often, this is a matter of stepping back, taking a look, and asking questions like "How could I make this better?" and "What is happening right now that is standing in the way of someone experiencing a Moment of Magic, and how could we keep that problem from happening again?" Let me give you an example of how posing such questions at Shepard Presentations helped us get closer to customers and serve them better.

One day, we got a call from a client who told us a book that he had ordered from us had not arrived. We told him we would look into it right away. After a little checking, we found that we had shipped the book out on time, yet the shipping service we used had failed to deliver the package. It didn't really matter why the book wasn't delivered. The point was, the book didn't show up. It was somewhere other than where it was supposed to be, and even though that wasn't our fault, it was now a problem that we had a responsibility to fix. (See Habit No. 4, *Amazing People Take Personal Responsibility*.)

We called the client back and said, "Here's what happened. Apparently, when we shipped this book, our shipping company lost it, and we really feel terrible about that. We're going to overnight you another book today. Here's the tracking number." The client came away pleased with how quickly we'd handled the situation.

Then, not even a month later, a similar problem happened again with another client. This time, however, the package had made it through to the right address, so it wasn't a shipping problem. We were able to confirm that someone at the client's location had signed for the package. It just never made it to the client's desk.

Just as we had done before, we called the client, explained what had happened, and sent a replacement book. Once again, it wasn't our fault, but we took full responsibility. Again, the client was happy with the outcome. While this type of problem didn't happen often, it happened enough for us to ask ourselves, "How can we keep this from happening in the future?"

That's the critical proactive question.

So we had a company meeting and made a decision to put a new process in place. We knew we weren't going to be able to be as automated as Amazon, but we did come up with something that worked well for us and for our customers. The process we implemented looks like this:

1. Somebody places an order.

2. We fulfill the order.

3. Once that's done, we send a thank-you message.

4. As part of that thank-you message, we include the tracking number so the client can track the shipment.

5. Three days later, we check the tracking number ourselves and make sure that the product has in fact arrived.

6. If it hasn't, we immediately inform the client.

7. If it has, we immediately inform the client. (Read this last one again. Notice that either way, we inform the client.)

With that thank-you message, our customer can track the order with the shipping number we provide. In addition, we check the status of the delivery. So even if there's a problem, the client doesn't have to be the one who spots it or reports it. Everybody benefits.

That's proactivity. That's spotting a pattern, noticing a potential negative impact that connects to that pattern, and then taking the initiative to make sure that the negative impact doesn't affect the customer. The examples in the next part of the book will give you some deeper insights into how that's done.

- **Remember: People do business with people.** Companies don't solve problems. People do.

- **Proactivity creates Amazement.** When you spot the long-term impact of problems left unaddressed and create processes that minimize those impacts, you lay the foundation for building Amazing relationships.

- **Proactivity overlaps with accountability.** Take responsibility for the situation, even if it isn't your fault. If you choose a company to ship a package, and the shipping company loses it, remember who chose the shipping company.

THINK AHEAD

Look around the corner. See what's coming. Anticipate what's next so you can stay a step ahead.

AMAZING PEOPLE THINK AHEAD.

Not just one step ahead. Amazing people think *several steps* ahead of what's happening right now. That's why we value them so much and want to be sure they get into our circle and stay in our circle. They help us deal with what's on the horizon.

A while back, I was interviewing someone for an opening at my company. One of the interview questions I posed was, "What's your definition of the perfect personal assistant?" Without missing a beat, this woman replied, "Radar O'Reilly."

You might not remember Radar O'Reilly. On the classic TV sitcom *M*A*S*H* (1972–1983), Radar was the habitually perceptive aide-de-camp to the mobile military hospital's commanding officer. He was famous for anticipating requests from his boss, and he was so good at doing it that he often announced the solution to a seemingly impossible problem before the boss even finished describing it. He was really, really good at anticipating what was needed next. Radar was always at least a step ahead of the boss, sometimes two or three steps ahead.

That job candidate gave me a great answer, one that led to a job offer. Ever since that discussion, Radar O'Reilly has been, for me, the perfect symbol for truly proactive working relationships.

For that matter, you could also offer the man who called himself Minnesota Fats as a role model when it comes to thinking ahead. Unless you're a student of pool or of film history, the name Minnesota Fats may not mean that much to you. Suffice it to say that this man, born Rudolf Wanderone, was perhaps the most famous pool player of all time. The character of the same name, played by Jackie Gleason in the classic 1961 Paul Newman film *The Hustler*, earned Gleason an Academy Award.

Minnesota Fats once told a reporter that he never just looked at the next shot. Instead, he always looked at the next *five* shots he was going to have to make. That's the kind of mindset I'm talking about. Similarly, the best chess players in the world don't just think about the next move. They think about the next *five to ten* moves. Some of them can even anticipate what the whole end game is going to look like once they make a certain move.

In a similar vein, Wayne Gretzky once said, "I skate to where the puck is going to be, not where it has been." In a game as fast as hockey, that means thinking well beyond the action of the present moment.

I believe Amazement is not just a matter of being one step ahead. It's about looking toward the end game of the challenges the people who count on us are likely to face. The question is, are we willing and able to get into the habit of thinking a few moves ahead on behalf of our customers and colleagues?

If this seems like a stretch, let me pose a question. When you go on a vacation, do you plan ahead by booking the right flight, with the right airline, to the right destination, or do you show up at the airport assuming that you'll be able to buy a ticket to the right place?

When your plane lands, do you know which hotel you'll be staying at, or do you wander out of the airport in search of a hotel that looks nice, hoping to find a decent place to stay that night?

You get the point. When we plan a vacation, we think several steps ahead. The people who count on us deserve the same level of attention and care.

By the way, I do realize that sometimes it can be fun to live without in-depth planning, not knowing quite where you'll go or what you'll do next. But in business—and this is a book about building business relationships and instilling confidence in those relationships—that kind of spontaneous approach is usually *not* the best way to create a sense that you are a cutting-edge contributor who consistently adds value to others. To earn that reputation, you have to plan ahead.

We must understand why people decide to work with us in the first place. That's our starting point. Then it's all about looking around corners, wondering "What if," and figuring out what customers and others are likely to want from us in the future, maybe even before they figure it out themselves. This way of looking at business relationships connects to a certain entrepreneurial vision that was perhaps best expressed by Apple cofounder Steve Jobs, who said, "It's really hard to design products by focus groups. A lot of times, people don't know what they want until you show it to them."

While this may be an extreme example, it makes the point. Steve Jobs was usually *more* than just a step ahead of the marketplace. If he hadn't been, his customers might never have gotten the iPhone or the iPad. These were revolutionary technologies that came into being only because someone was willing to think ahead and ask, "What if...?"

- **Plan ahead.** Whether you're thinking just one step ahead, or five, or ten, the goal of being forward thinking—of anticipating and addressing needs ahead of time—will create deeper confidence in all your business relationships.

- **Identify problems others are likely to have to deal with.** What specific challenges are they going to face tomorrow, next week, next month, or next year?

- **Ask "What if...?"** Try to figure out what people who count on you are likely to want from you in the future, even if *they're* not sure yet.

CREATE A PREDICTABLY POSITIVE EXPERIENCE

Any loss in consistency lowers the level of trust in the relationship and undermines the loyalty of the person who has chosen to work with us.

NOT LONG AGO, MY wife and I went out to dinner at a restaurant in Saint Louis, where we live. The service we received was quite good, and the food was excellent. But something happened during the meal that might make us hesitate before going back.

As we were being seated, I noticed one of the other guests had a delicious-looking entrée. I asked the server about it, and he said it was jambalaya, a spicy Cajun rice dish with sausage and shrimp. It looked delicious, so I ordered it. When it came out, I noticed that my dish had less rice and more sauce than the other diner's plate. Not only that, there was a larger amount of seafood on mine. It looked quite different from the other guest's entrée.

The owner came over and asked how we were enjoying our meal. I commented on how delicious the food was. (It really was.) I also mentioned that my plate had more sauce than expected. I wasn't complaining. I was actually complimenting the chef, or so I thought.

The owner went on to tell me that the kitchen staff was a bit overworked that day, as there was a special event that was causing them a little stress in the kitchen. The jambalaya I had seen at the other table, she explained, was more typical of what guests usually got, which had both less sauce and less seafood. It was as though she expected me to be happy about the "bonus" I had received. But I wasn't. Let me explain why.

In effect, the restaurant owner was saying that when it gets busy at the restaurant, the customers can't expect consistency. This time, because the process was a little unpredictable, my dinner had been a bit better than what was to be expected. In her view, I should consider myself lucky. That's probably not the message she wanted me to hear, but that's how I took it.

Here's a question. What happens if I come back next time and order the same dish, and it comes out the way it is *supposed* to be prepared? I'll certainly notice the difference. I might wonder why there isn't as much of the delicious seafood they gave me the last time I ordered the dish. I might say something to the server or owner about that.

And then, before I even leave the restaurant, I might begin to wonder what I am likely to get when I come back the *next* time—and because I'm not sure, I decide not to come back at all.

My challenge was not so much with the process the restaurant owner put in place for creating jambalaya— that's her business and her responsibility. My challenge was with her assumption that customers don't care if the experience is consistent. We do. When we buy a can of Coca-Cola in Saint Louis, we want it to be the same as the can of Coca-Cola we had in Kansas City. We are drawn to a "no surprises" experience.

By accident, that restaurant owner created a false expectation. Even though the meal was great, she left herself open to the negative experience I call service roulette—a syndrome in which people don't know what to expect from you and lose confidence in you and your business as a result.

When you commit to a "no surprises" standard, both personally and as an organization, you lay the foundation for an ever-deepening level of trust in all your professional relationships. You take on the personal responsibility for setting up systems and processes that keep customers, colleagues, and others from ever having to wonder, *Hmm, what am I going to get next time?*

In short, you embrace the Loyalty Formula:

Good Service + Consistency = Potential Loyalty

Notice that I said, "potential loyalty." Any loss in consistency threatens the trust in the relationship and, thus, the loyalty of the person who has chosen to work with us.

Look at it this way. People do business with those whom they like and trust. "Like" is the easy part—I liked the meal I got at that restaurant. The food and service were good, and the owner was very pleasant. "Trust" is a little trickier to earn. I didn't trust the restaurant to deliver the same experience again, and as a result, I'm less likely to recommend that friends and family go there or go back for a second time myself.

- **There must be a predictably positive experience.** The surest way to confuse people and make them lose confidence in you and your business is to expect them to embrace an inconsistent experience.

- **Follow the Loyalty Formula (Good Service + Consistency = Potential Loyalty).** If we *consistently* deliver the desired experience, people will not only like working with us but also gain a sense of trust that they can expect to receive the same experience the next time.

- **Consistency takes hard work and a lot of planning, but it is worth it.** The result is that you create trust and confidence.

THINK OUTSIDE THE RULE BOOK

Think of the relationship before you start reciting the rule book.

A LITTLE EARLIER, I shared some thoughts on the importance of building a culture within your organization that avoids the word *no* in interactions with people who are counting on you. Now it's time to take a closer look at exactly how that's supposed to happen.

When I talk with businesspeople about avoiding the word *no*, I sometimes get pushback. A common question I often hear is, "What about the rules and policies?"

There is an old saying: "Rules are made to be broken." Now, a lot of management experts recoil in horror when they hear that. They insist that this is an idea that doesn't really work in the world of business. They're right—but only up to a point. When it comes to our most important business relationships, which include our relationships with customers, there should definitely be rules. However, there are very few hard-and-fast rules that can never, ever be broken. The rest can and should be broken when circumstances warrant.

What we have here is an opportunity for an important discussion about two very different ways of looking at our interactions with customers and others who count on us. We have to decide whether we are approaching these people from an *operations* focus or from a *relationship* focus. The first way of interacting with people is about following the rules; the second way is about connecting with the person. Amazing teams and companies always lean toward the second way.

Doing the right thing for the relationship is sometimes different than following the rules. This idea may take some time for us to get used to if we've built a career or a company around being operations focused, but it's an important idea for us to accept if we're serious about building an Amazing culture. I'm talking about building the kind of culture that actively takes the initiative and looks for alternatives to rules and policies that could negatively impact the customer. Another word to describe this is *flexibility*.

By the way, when you're relationship focused, that doesn't mean you assume that all rules are meant to be broken. There are, in my experience, five really important rules that can never, ever be broken. Everyone in the organization has to know about them and follow them. Here they are:

1. Don't lie to me. (Integrity in communication is essential.)

2. Don't steal from me. (If you can't agree to this, you can't work here.)

3. Don't do something that's illegal. (Ditto.)

4. Don't do something that is going to hurt my business. (Ditto.)

5. Don't do something that you know is going to upset the customer, your fellow employee, or one of our business partners. If you feel you have no choice, talk to a supervisor about the situation. (This is just common sense.)

Those are five rules that most employers would consider to be foundational. But you know what? Anything that falls outside of these five is potentially a place where we need to learn to be flexible and think outside the rule book. When the opportunity presents itself, and we know that breaking a rule is going to help a relationship, we *can* break those lesser rules. And there are going to be times we should.

Great companies, Amazing companies, embrace this principle. They literally encourage their employees to break the lesser rules—when doing so serves the customer and the company.

Knowing when breaking a lesser rule serves the company is the difference between the leadership mindset and the employee mindset. That's a transition that may not happen as easily for some people on the team as it does for others, but it's got to happen. We need to draw a clear line between being focused on operations and being focused on the relationship. Operations-focused people do the job without deviating from the norm. Relationship-focused people understand what the job is and realize that serving people is the whole reason they are in business. They are oriented toward finding solutions, they are flexible, and they understand that in most cases, rules are really just guidelines.

"Freedom is not worth having if it does not include the freedom to make mistakes."

—MAHATMA GANDHI

People who are trained properly should be given clear examples of times when it makes sense to break lesser rules. They get the answer to the question, "What do I do if I encounter such and such a situation?" But just as important, they are given something else: permission to think. They know what the five big unbreakable rules are, and they know they can't step over any of those lines. Not only that, they know just how close they should get to them, which will vary by situation. This is a matter of ongoing training and reinforcement. Everyone should know how far they can go in service of the relationship.

Here's a great example of what thinking outside the rule book looks like in action. Recently, I was working with a major auto manufacturer. I was talking to the twenty-five specialized customer service reps who are ultimately responsible for addressing serious complaints that haven't been resolved at lower levels of the company. All of those twenty-five people even have the authority to buy back a car from an unhappy consumer. If the situation gets so bad that that's the best way forward, they all know they can offer to buy back the car in order to salvage a relationship with a customer who has a problem for which the company is responsible.

So how many times do you think one of those managers has actually bought back a car from a consumer over the past five years?

Here's the answer: Zero. But the point is, they know they can, and that affects the culture and the decision-making process.

- **Learn and share the importance of relationship-focused thinking.** If you happen to be a manager, give people the freedom to do the right thing for both the customer and the company. Teach them how to think creatively and come up with alternative solutions.

- **Learn to ask these questions:** Is this customer's request really unreasonable? Is it going to hurt the company in any way? Will it compromise profit? Is it illegal or will it cause harm to anybody? (If the answer to any of those questions is yes, don't do it.) Is there a substitute that could meet or even exceed the original expectations?

- **Learn to trust your customers.** Too many rules are designed to manage the tiny minority of dishonest people. If people want to cheat or steal from you, they will figure out a way to do so. Do you want to create rules for the 1 percent (or less) of people you *don't* want to do business with, or do you want to create an environment that focuses on people you *do* want coming back again and again?

STAY A STEP AHEAD

Create a process that solves problems—before others ever find out there was a problem.

A WHILE BACK, MY mobile phone rang. I didn't recognize the number.

I answered the call and found myself talking to Jill, an American Express customer service representative. Jill was calling to ask me to verify some recent charges that had shown up on my account. She explained that there was an unusual purchase pattern. It looked as if my card might have been compromised; could she and I talk for a few minutes about whether there had been fraudulent charges in the past twelve hours?

Of course I agreed to this. Sure enough, after just a couple of questions, we determined that there were in fact about a dozen charges from the other side of the world that I had not made. Somehow—who knows how—

somebody had obtained my credit card details and was on a spending spree.

Jill assured me that I would not be responsible for any of those charges. She then informed me that she would make sure that the account was closed and that I would receive another card within the next twenty-four hours. When I mentioned that I was going to be out of town that evening, staying at a hotel for a speech I was scheduled to give the next morning, that didn't deter Jill at all. She simply asked if it would be OK to send the card to the hotel. I said yes. She confirmed that the card would be waiting for me at the front desk by 10:30 a.m. or sooner.

Here is what makes this a great lesson in Amazement:

1. Jill was proactive in solving my problem, which of course means that American Express was proactive in solving my problem. Had they not taken the initiative, I wouldn't have known the problem existed until my next bill came. By then, who knows how much might have been illegally charged to my credit card. I might not have been liable for all those charges but untangling them all would have been a major inconvenience. And the longer the unauthorized card was out there, the more chance I had of running into problems like this again.

2. My problem became Jill's problem. Notice that her *personal* proactivity was what led me to decide that

American Express *as a whole* was proactive. She, as a representative of the company, took full ownership of the problem. I didn't have to do anything but accept her help and support.

3. Jill came up with an immediate solution. She had a plan in place to get me a replacement card. When she found out I wasn't going to be at home on the day the card was delivered, she modified the plan in a way that worked for me.

Sometimes people will "dump" bad news in another person's lap and then make that person responsible for coming up with a solution. For instance, think of a work colleague who e-mails you the day before he heads off for vacation, saying something like, "This report needs more meat" but doesn't offer any guidance on what "more meat" actually means. Does your colleague mean additional examples that back up the report's central idea? Does he mean more *new* ideas? Does he mean more formal citations to outside sources that will support the report's conclusion? You have no clue what his vague message meant, and because the report is due next week, it's now your job to figure it out.

That kind of dumping is not what happened when my credit card number was stolen. Never for an instant did I feel like I was the one who was on the hook for dealing with this situation. Jill reached out to tell me about the problem, and just as important, Jill was taking the lead in solving the problem.

Now here's the really cool part. This is "business as usual" for American Express. What I figured out shortly after the call was that American Express does this every day for its cardholders, who are also known as members. People like Jill make calls like this all the time, and they stop little card theft problems before they become bigger problems. They have a system and procedures in place to protect members, and that's reassuring.

That's more than customer service. That's confidence creation.

Confidence doesn't happen by accident. It has to be designed and executed as a process. For someone to have confidence in a company, the company's product or service has to work, the company's people have to create a great service experience, and the experience has to be consistent and predictable. It has to be good all of the time, not some of the time. The goal is for the customer to "own" the experience. When I can count on the experience to be consistently better than average (as mine was with Jill—and every other time I've interacted with American Express), the company is operating in the zone of Amazement.

After a number of above-average experiences, the people on the receiving end of those experiences start saying things like, "They're *always* on top of things." "They *always* look out for you." "They're *always* a step ahead." Whenever you start hearing the word *always* followed by something positive, you know there's a process in place that supports Amazement.

American Express *amazed* me because Jill took the initiative. Jill took the initiative because American Express set up a procedure that gave her the tools she needed to be proactive in creating a solution to my problem—a problem I didn't even know existed.

Yes, it takes time and effort to set up a process that allows you to take the initiative on behalf of your most important business relationships. However, it takes even more time and effort to deal with the problems that result from *not* having such a process.

Creating a process for staying a step ahead of a problem and reaching out first is a great way to build and maintain trust in your relationships with customers and everyone else.

So don't just announce or "dump" bad news and leave the other person responsible for dealing with a problem. Create a process that allows you and your team to stay a step ahead of the difficulties that the people who are counting on you face. Reach out first, and take responsibility when there's a problem.

- **Be proactive.** Take the initiative early, and reach out the moment you know there's a problem.

- **Be accountable.** Once you identify the challenge or

problem, even if it is not your problem, be accountable for owning and delivering the solution. Don't "dump" the issue in the other person's lap. Let him or her know it's your issue to resolve.

- **Create a process that lets you stay a step ahead.** This creates confidence and trust.

KEY TAKEAWAYS FOR THE SECOND HABIT: AMAZING PEOPLE ARE PROACTIVE

- Don't blame others for what you have control over. Even if it isn't your fault, take responsibility.

- Try to figure out what customers and others who count on you are likely to want from you in the future, even if they're not sure yet.

- The Loyalty Formula: Good Service + Consistency = Potential Loyalty

- Learn to trust your customers. Most people are honest, but too many businesses and people create rules designed to manage the small percentage of dishonest people.

- Create a process that lets you stay a step ahead. This creates confidence and trust.

THE THIRD HABIT:

AMAZING PEOPLE WANT FEEDBACK

ASK DIRECTLY FOR FEEDBACK

If you think you don't need to hear constructive criticism, you're the person who needs it the most.

AMAZING PEOPLE AND ORGANIZATIONS want feedback.

They don't hide from criticism, positive or negative. They relish it. They view complaints as gifts, as opportunities to improve. They see any criticism as a chance to learn something new, either about themselves or the person with whom they're dealing. They always want a performance review, formal or otherwise, because they want to know exactly how they're doing. If there's a problem, they want to know about it. If they're doing well, they want to know how they can continue to do well—or preferably, do a little better.

If your goal is to deliver a consistently above-average

experience to the people who trust you and rely on you, it stands to reason that you would want to know what those people think about how you're doing—*otherwise, you'll never know for sure.* In your mind, you may believe you're delivering an above-average experience. But the real-world results may be very different, and you need to know what the other person's actual responses are to what you did. If there's a problem, it's better to course-correct sooner rather than later.

Amazing people embrace the feedback they get, and then they do something with it. Anything less than that could cost them their job, a customer, or a relationship.

Of course, this is all part of a larger strategy of creating a vibrant, engaged, loyal community of advocates and allies. You're looking for any and every idea from anyone who will help you to improve. If you look closely at truly successful people and teams, you'll see that they are all eager to get that kind of feedback.

For instance, software and technology companies launch user groups in which people come together to discuss how to best use certain products. Leaders at those companies are focused on creating a better experience and a better end result, based on the feedback they get from these groups. Some of that feedback can be very frank. You can be certain that big enterprises like Apple, Adobe, and Google make absolutely sure that preliminary users have had a chance to share their uncensored insights on how a new application works—or doesn't—before they roll out a new release to the public. They want to hear as much criticism as they possibly can before the big launch, and they want to act on that criticism to create a better product, better communications about the product, and a better user experience.

Many people I've worked with over the years have asked me whether it's a nonnegotiable rule to seek out and listen to critical feedback on a regular basis.

This question always reminds me of a famous sports photo of the legendary golfer Tiger Woods. The photo shows Woods in his prime, working on his game with his coach, Butch Harmon. It always impressed me that a world-class athlete, someone who at the time was number one in the world, would still seek advice and feedback from a coach.

Tiger Woods knew what every truly great athlete, executive, and performer knows—namely, that there is no individual success big enough to justify tuning out critical feedback. We *all* need feedback on how we can improve, and sometimes the feedback that sounds the most negative is the feedback we most need to hear. Sometimes that feedback comes from a coach. Sometimes it comes from a customer—or a colleague or a friend you respect. Whatever the source, we are well advised to listen to it closely. We may choose not to act on it, but we won't be able to tell whether that feedback is constructive unless we first listen to it.

- **Ask for feedback.** Spend time eliciting feedback from customers, colleagues, vendors, a coach, or anyone else you choose.

- **Listen without prejudice.** Open your eyes and ears to all feedback—the good, the bad, and the ugly.

- **Find the constructive criticism.** You may not act on all the criticism you receive, but listen to every piece of criticism you can. Some of it will be constructive and useful.

LOOK PAST THE HONEYMOON

Make sure people who count on you continue to have their expectations met—not just today but tomorrow, too.

THIS IS AN OLD story, I know, and maybe one with which you're already familiar. I share it here to make an important point about Amazement.

Once upon a time, a man named Jim died and went to heaven.

As it turned out, Jim had led an exemplary life. When he got to the Pearly Gates, the attendant on duty tipped his cap, smiled, and said, "Congratulations, Jim. You've earned a choice. You get to choose where you want to stay for the rest of eternity—here or the Place Downstairs."

"Really?"

"Yep. It's entirely up to you. You get to take a tour of both Heaven and the Place Downstairs. But make your choice carefully. Once you decide, there's no changing your mind."

"Fair enough," Jim said. "Where do I start?"

"With me," said the attendant. "Let's get started. I'll show you around Heaven."

Heaven was lovely. The gardens were well maintained, and the people seemed cheerful. The attendant asked him, "What do you think?"

Heaven looked OK to Jim, but he couldn't help wondering whether, maybe, just maybe, Heaven was a little... boring. He thought of the garden clubs, the shuffleboard tournaments, the cookouts. There was nothing wrong with any of that. Still, he was curious about how the tour of the other place was going to go.

"Well, we're done with my tour," the attendant said. "Now it's time for the Other Guy to show you the Place Downstairs." With those words, he vanished. Suddenly, Jim was looking at a very different place: sleek, clean, colorful, and brimming with energy and activity. It was like a combination of a nightclub and a really cool resort.

Everywhere he looked, Jim liked what he saw. People were dancing. People were singing. People were working out. Dozens of different parties were going on, and every single party was Jim's party.

Suddenly, he was back at the gates of Heaven. The moment came for Jim to make his choice. As tactfully as he could, he told the attendant who had given him the first tour that he was choosing to spend eternity in the Place Downstairs.

The moment he said that, Jim was whisked to a dark and very scary place where he was immediately chained to a stone wall and told, "Here is where you will spend eternity."

The next day, Jim saw the Other Guy. "Hey!" Jim shouted from the hard stone wall where he'd been chained up all night. "When I took the tour with you yesterday, there was nothing but singing and dancing and parties around here. Now I'm chained up to this wall. Where are the parties? Where are the people? What happened?"

"That's easy to answer," the Other Guy said with a delicate, sly grin. "Yesterday, you were a prospect. Today, you're a customer."

The moral of this story is pretty simple: In every relationship, there is a honeymoon phase. If you're in sales, this could be before the prospect becomes a customer. If you're in management, the honeymoon period could be the first month after a new employee joins your team. At some point, though, things become familiar and comfortable, and reality starts to surface. At that point, the honeymoon is over, and people begin to take one another for granted. But that doesn't mean they should.

If you're going to find out what people think (and you should), make sure that ongoing "How are we doing?" questions are part of the relationship itself, not just part of the so-called honeymoon period. The trouble with honeymoon periods is that they have a way of ending too soon. Please don't make the mistake of thinking this story is only about customer relationships. It's not. It's about everyone you work with, everyone you count on, and everyone who counts on you.

- **Don't take customers or anyone else for granted.** If someone is counting on you, that person deserves your best efforts.

- **What people see should be what they get from us.** What they experience when they decide to work with us should be what they get during the entire business relationship.

- **Look beyond the honeymoon period.** We need to keep seeking out feedback, asking for insights, and checking in on how the other person thinks we're doing—and keep acting on that feedback all of the time.

RATE YOURSELF

If you don't measure the quality of the experience you deliver, you can't possibly improve it.

IT WAS EITHER PETER Drucker or W. Edwards Deming who said, "You can't manage what you don't measure." Whoever said it first, he was absolutely right. If you don't know whether the needle is going up or down, you can only guess whether what you're doing is delivering value for the other person or not.

Sometimes when people hear me speaking about quantifying the value delivered, they assume I'm talking about implementing all kinds of intricate calculations, surveys, and spreadsheets to measure performance. Actually, rating yourself can be very simple. Personally, I'm a firm believer in asking the people who count on me a simple 1-to-10 question. It might sound like this:

Based on your experience so far, I'm curious. On a scale of 1 to 10, how would you rate what I'm doing?

Ask this question often. Write down and date the answers you receive. If you get anything less than 10, be prepared to ask an important follow-up question.

Let's say you get a 4. Try asking this:

"I'm curious, what would it take for me to get a 5?"

And if you get a 5, ask:

"I'm curious, what would it take for me to get a 6?"

Here's why this is important. When you ask this kind of question, some people will give you a 10, which is great, of course. But some people will give you a score that's *less* than a 10 out of 10, because they feel there's room for improvement. You want to know where and how to make that improvement. The problem is, though, the number they share with you may not be all that meaningful, because you don't know the "why" behind it. So once you know the number, you can get a better understanding by asking what it takes to get a single number higher. This is a critical reality check. Don't skip it.

Measuring satisfaction on a 1-to-10 scale is an idea that's been around more or less forever. The most current example of this kind of question is the popular Net Promoter Score®, which is the result of asking someone how likely he or she is to recommend you to others, on a 0-to-10 scale. Although that's the start of a potentially useful conversation, you must seek to understand the reason behind the number. Again, if you *don't* get a 10 out of 10, ask the person what you need to do to get a point higher.

Here are some other follow-ups for the Net Promoter Score® question that I've shared over the years.

"Why did you give me that score?"

"Is there one thing you can think of that would make your experience of working with us better?"

(If you didn't get a 9 or a 10) "I'm just curious, why didn't we get a 9 or a 10?"

Again, keep track of the answers, monitor them over time, and find ways to improve. You might even consider sharing the responses you receive with the people who help you to deliver value.

Once you're officially measuring your performance and based on what you learn, you can set new performance standards that make it likelier for people to want to keep working with you and sing your praises to others. You've started an important conversation about improving over time, and you've demonstrated that you're personally committed to delivering an Amazing experience. You're perfectly positioned to create an ongoing dialogue about long-term growth, improvement, and innovation.

· **Ask people who count on you to rate your performance on a scale of 1 to 10.** Then, if necessary, ask what it will take to a score a point higher.

· **Ask about how to make the experience better.** A particularly powerful question to ask someone who counts on you is, "What's one thing I could do to make the experience of working with us better?"

- **Set a new standard.** Use what you learn from discussions about how you could do better to set a new performance benchmark, one that makes it likelier for people to want to keep working with you.

FULFILL THE PROMISE

Create—and keep—your personal brand promise.

THERE ARE MANY GOOD definitions of the word *brand*. One of my favorites is:

"A brand is a promise delivered."

Notice that there's no distinction in that definition about who's *making* the promise. The promise maker behind the brand can be a company, a nonprofit organization, or even an individual. If you make a promise, and you then follow through to the satisfaction of the person or people you made the promise to, that's your brand. It's a pretty simple concept. As I've noted earlier, it is other people who determine whether you *kept* your promise. Their perception is their reality.

So consider: Apple, one of the leading technology companies in the world, has a world-famous brand promise that says, "Think different." That's a powerful, compelling two-word challenge that carries all kinds of interesting implications. What does Apple's famous slogan do? Well, for one thing, it tells everyone who hears it about the possibility of living a certain kind of life—a life where old assumptions can and should be challenged and where conformity for its own sake is set aside.

Maybe you're wondering, *What makes this a promise?* Two things. First, with that short, deceptively simple-sounding sentence, Apple is promising to offer us products that help us to see and interact with the world in new, different, and exciting ways—products that help us to "think different." And second, it's promising to help each of us operate in the world as a special kind of person, the kind of person who questions assumptions, who moves past old ideas, who brings new perspectives to life and new solutions to problems. That one sentence, just two words long, inspires us by promising to help us transform *ourselves*. With those two words, Apple is promising to help make us more creative, more inquisitive, more innovative. Apple is promising to give us tools that will help us *become* someone who thinks differently.

What I want you to notice is that Apple's brand promise is aspirational, and it backs up its aspirational promise with superb listening. Apple is one of the best companies in the world when it comes to listening to its customers about how well it's fulfilling its promise. The company is constantly eliciting feedback from individual customers, members of user groups, and people who volunteer to beta test its products and services. Apple has truly great communication with its customers and prospective customers, and that communication helps its leadership keep an eye on how people around the world feel about whether or not they are living up to that exceptionally powerful brand promise.

Maybe you've noticed that many Apple users are enthusiastic evangelists for Apple. The reason: For them, the "think different" brand promise has been fulfilled. Now, most of us are used to thinking about *companies* having brands. We may even be attuned to our own company's brand, and we may be working hard to support it. It may be a little more difficult, though, for us to remember that each of us also has a *personal* brand—a promise we make to those with whom we work and live. It's in our best interest that we:

1. Make our personal brand promise a conscious choice

2. Ensure that it lines up with the team's and/or company's brand promise

3. Solicit feedback regularly about how well our colleagues, customers, and critical business contacts feel we are doing in keeping that promise

Most people I work with haven't yet identified their own personal, aspirational brand promise. When I explain what a brand promise is and ask what theirs is, they say things like, "I never thought about that." If that's your response right now to what you're reading, let me ask you: What's the promise you make as an individual to those who work with you? What *should* the promise you make to them be? The answer you come up with should illuminate not only "Why I come to work every day" but also "Why I work *here*."

As an example, our company's goal is to *Always be Amazing*. That's our brand promise as an organization and mine as an individual. I not only try to deliver on it but also ask people how I'm doing at fulfilling that promise. I ask people to tell me how close I am coming to meeting the standard of always being Amazing. If there's a problem, I want them to tell me face-to-face, to pick up the phone, or send me an e-mail. And if there's a success, of course I want to hear how people feel about that as well. I tell customers, employees, and stakeholders, "What you get from me should be Amazing. This is me. This is who I am. This is what I am committed to: Amazement. I really hope you'll tell me if I hit the mark for you."

And as much as I love it to receive confirmation and accolades about being Amazing, I also love to hear when someone has a suggestion on how I can improve. It gives me important information I need if I'm going to do an even better job of delivering on my personal brand promise.

- **Amazing people commit to a personal brand.** They make sure that their brand aligns with the team's and company's brand, and they ask those with whom they work how they're doing in fulfilling their brand promise.

- **Ask yourself, "What do I commit to being at work (or in any important relationship)?"** That's worth taking some time to figure out. The answer you come back with should be personal and aspirational and tell people what your working life is about.

- **Share your personal vision and your vision for others.** Make sure they are both in alignment.

COMMIT TO CONSTANT, NEVER-ENDING IMPROVEMENT

Always be on the lookout for new ways to Amaze.

I CLOSE OUT THIS third section of the book by challenging you to pose a critical (and perhaps familiar) question: *How can we get better?*

The feedback we get may come in the form of an explicit suggestion. Or it may take the form of an exchange that sparks an idea about how you can move to a whole new level of excellence, a level of constant, never-ending improvement that supports you, your team and/or organization, and everyone who relies on you. You may experience a sudden moment of insight about this "How can we get better?" question while you are interacting with someone who is counting on you, without the person even saying anything. That's the best kind of feedback there is. When this happens, you want to notice it and follow through appropriately.

I wrote an article recently about a segment on the *CBS Sunday Morning* TV show that featured an extraordinary story about someone who noticed, and acted on, such an opportunity for excellence. She got feedback from someone who wasn't trying to say a word.

Krystal Payne, who worked at a Starbucks in Leesburg, Virginia, noticed that one of her regular customers, a gentleman by the name of Ibby Piracha, was deaf. Interacting with him as he placed his order was not as easy as it could have been. Krystal thought, *How can we get better?*, and came up with an Amazing solution.

The next time Ibby came to get his usual coffee, Krystal used sign language to take his order. She handed him a handwritten note. It read:

I've been learning ASL, American Sign Language, just so you can have the same experience as everyone else.

Krystal had taken three hours of her own time to go on the Internet to find information about ASL, just so she could use sign language to ask a single customer what he wanted to drink. But her actions affected many more people than herself and Ibby. Krystal commented to the reporter, "If he's a regular, and I want to make that connection with my regulars, I should be able to at least ask him what he wants to drink."

This is a great story to share and learn from. I took away at least three big lessons from it.

First and foremost, Krystal Payne is obviously an exceptional person. She is personally focused on the question, "How can we get better?" And she looks for answers to that question in places that a lot of other people wouldn't look. She understands what Amazement is all about. She gets people. Nobody told her to go home and learn sign language. Nobody offered to pay her to do it. She did it simply because she knew it was the right thing to do. She knew it would make somebody else's experience better.

Second, Starbucks hired her. Working for Starbucks is a good job. They don't take everyone who simply applies.

Third, Krystal set an example for everyone else. At that moment, even though she wasn't a manager, she demonstrated incredible leadership qualities. When I say "leader," what I mean is someone driven by aspiration, someone willing to ask, "What will make this better for everyone?"

Have you noticed that some people just do what they are supposed to do and no more? When someone finds a way to pose, and act on, the question "How can we get better?," that person will always stand out. Why? Because people notice when others exceed their expectations.

- **Ask yourself, "How can I (or we) get better?"** If you make a habit of posing that question, day after day, you can transform yourself and your organization.

- **Anybody can be average or just OK.** It's the excellent people who make a difference. They do that by asking themselves what it takes to exceed expectations.

- **Sometimes people don't have to say anything for you to recognize an opportunity to improve.** Always be on the lookout for new ways to Amaze.

KEY TAKEAWAYS FOR THE THIRD HABIT: AMAZING PEOPLE WANT FEEDBACK

- Find a way to spend time with and get feedback from people who are counting on you.

- Don't take customers—or anyone else—for granted.

- Ask people who count on you to rate your performance on a scale of 1 to 10. If you don't earn a 10, find out why.

- Define your personal brand. Share it with those in your circle. It should explain not just why you come to work each day, but also why you *choose* to do the work you do.

- Excellent people and companies make a difference by constantly asking, "How can we get better?"

AMAZING PEOPLE TAKE PERSONAL RESPONSIBILITY

OWN IT! TAKE PERSONAL RESPONSIBILITY

Never duck responsibility. Make absolutely sure it stops with you.

A FEW YEARS BACK, I wrote a book titled *Amaze Every Customer Every Time*. I was, and am, proud of the book. I'm also proud of my partnership with Ace Hardware. Ace was the source of the dozens of case studies that gave rise to the book's fifty-two tools for delivering Amazing service. Ace Hardware is, by the way, one of the truly great customer-centered enterprises on the planet. That's not why I am telling you about *Amaze Every Customer Every Time*, though.

I'm telling you about this book because, when I

launched it in 2013, I set up a special presale offer for people who ordered the book before it was released to the public. The idea was simple. If you ordered the book in advance, you not only got the hardbound book mailed on the release date, but you also got a free download of the e-book at the time you placed the order. This was a limited-time offer. As the name of the promotion suggested, the offer officially ended when the book came out.

Two years after that book launch, though, something interesting happened. One of our customers sent us an e-mail, providing proof of purchase of the physical book and requesting the free e-book. This customer was not weeks, not months, but *years* past the closing date of the promotion. We weren't even sure if the promotional code would still work. (It didn't.) It had been too long.

So what would you have done in that situation?

There's no one right answer, by the way. Before I tell you what we did, let me share with you what we *didn't* do.

We didn't cite policy at the customer by reminding him to read the formal terms of the promotion or by sending him off to check some website. We didn't send a vaguely worded form letter saying, "Thanks for reaching out, but we're unable to fulfill your request," in hopes that he'd lose interest (or simply decide he didn't have time to pursue the matter). And we didn't call the customer and ask, "Hey, have you checked a calendar recently? Did you notice that this was a *presale* promotion, not an *after-the-book-launched* promotion? Did you notice that it's been more than two years since this book came out? Have you got a clear sense of how time works, meaning in which direction it moves?"

I don't think any of those options crossed our minds. Why not? Because we were not trying to start or win an argument. That's not Amazing behavior.

What did we do? We shared the e-mail with one another, read it out loud, had a good laugh about the customer's assumption that the offer was still valid, and then asked ourselves, "OK. What's the best response to this situation?"

The answer we came back with was, "We should do what we'd want to have done for us in a similar situation."

We ended up deciding that if we were the customer, we'd prefer to see the company make the best effort it possibly could to live up to its word. All other things being equal, we believed personal accountability should drive the discussion. If we *could* find a way to live up to our word, without causing any undue problems or compromising any of our other commitments, we felt we *should* try to find a way to live up to what this customer expected.

And that's what we did.

We sent him a free e-book. We chose to *own* the customer's situation. And that's what I want to challenge you to do as you make your way through this section of the book. Do what Amazing people and teams do. Choose to be personally responsible, even when you can come up with plenty of reasons not to.

People remember that kind of choice.

- **The next time you find yourself in a challenging situation, look beyond who's right and who's wrong.** Ask yourself whether there's a way to do what you'd want done on your behalf in a similar situation.

- **Be accountable.** As long as you can do so without compromising your other commitments, assume responsibility for delivering on the other person's expectations.

- **Make good decisions that benefit others.** No, you won't always be able to exceed someone's expectations, but that doesn't mean you shouldn't try. If there are no downsides to giving the other person what he or she wants, make an effort to do it.

A COMMON PURPOSE

Know why you show up for work every day.

SOMETIMES, WHEN I TALK to people about personal accountability in the workplace, I'll ask a deceptively simple-sounding question:

> *What is the one purpose of your business that you are ALL personally accountable for supporting?*

I've heard a number of interesting answers to this question. For instance, sometimes people start reciting a mission statement or a sentence or two they've memorized about the company's values. If I hear that, I'll say something like:

> *"That's good to know—and it's important—but I'm not talking about your mission or your values. Let me put it another way. What one purpose is everyone in your*

organization accountable for supporting, regardless of the person's job title? What does everyone in your organization have in common?"

This generally produces an awkward silence. That's when I say:

"Believe it or not, everyone in your organization is personally accountable for supporting one single purpose—the purpose of your business.

"The purpose of your business—of any business—is to acquire and hold on to customers.

"Therefore, this is also the purpose of every employee of a business. That's it. That's what you're all here for. Ultimately, you are personally accountable for supporting that purpose, whether you are the CEO, working in the mailroom, or doing anything in between. If what you're accountable for doesn't support the goal of acquiring and holding on to customers, you aren't accountable for the right thing."

I've written about this concept at length in other books, and I've shared it in countless live speeches and training sessions. It's a core Amazement concept that I feel can't be emphasized enough. This idea of the purpose of a business being able to get and keep customers is not mine.

Theodore Levitt, senior professor at Harvard Business School, may have been the first to publish the concept in his book *Marketing Imagination*, and Peter Drucker may have helped to make it famous, but many, many people have shared this idea. It's something business leaders—and indeed entire organizations—need to grasp, share, and constantly reinforce up and down the organization.

It always surprises me how few CEOs and company founders are willing to hold themselves accountable to this purpose.

By the way, when I ask people what the purpose of a business is, the most common initial answer I hear is, "To make money."

For the record, making money is a *goal*. If you confuse the purpose with the goal, you may not reach your goal. But if you focus on customers, the money will follow.

- **Understand and share the true purpose of your business.** The purpose of your business is to acquire and keep customers.

- **Focus on customers and the money will follow.** Don't make the mistake of believing the purpose of your business is to make money. That's a goal. Getting and keeping customers is your purpose.

- **Look closely at what you do, day in and day out.** If what you are spending your time and resources on supports the purpose of getting and keeping customers, keep doing it. If it doesn't, make a change.

IT'S NOT MY FAULT, BUT NOW IT'S MY PROBLEM

Step up when things go wrong. It may not be your fault, but it is your opportunity to Amaze.

PERSONAL ACCOUNTABILITY MEANS TAKING ownership of the situation—whether it's going well or going poorly, and whether you had a role in creating the situation or are brand new to it. It means stepping up and saying, "This situation may not be my fault, but it is now my problem, and I'm responsible for fixing it." This is an essential trait of Amazing people, and it presents itself in some of the most unexpected places.

We're used to hearing about personal accountability as a trait of great managers and leaders, and it certainly is that. It's important to remember, though, that in the very best teams, *everyone* is willing to step up and be accountable, regardless of his or her job title or position on the organizational chart.

Here's a perfect example of what I mean. A while back, I was staying at a great hotel, the Embassy Suites in beautiful Portland, Oregon. I had a wonderful stay. On the day I was to check out, I had an important phone call scheduled. My plan was to head to the airport immediately after the call to catch my flight home. I knew I would be in a hurry after the call, so before I made the call, I went to the bell stand and talked to the doorman—his name was Arturo—to arrange to have a cab waiting for me at a specific time. Arturo said he would take care of it.

When I finished my call and walked out of the hotel at the arranged time, I noticed that there wasn't a taxi waiting. Guess what? Arturo noticed, too.

Was it Arturo's *fault* that my cab was late? Of course not.

Was it Arturo's *problem* that my cab was late? He seemed to think so.

Arturo called the cab company and found out that it would be at least ten or fifteen minutes before the cab would be there. Based on our earlier conversation, he knew how concerned I was about getting to the airport on time to make my flight. He looked me in the eye and responded, "Don't worry, I'll take you. Wait right here." Within moments, we were on our way.

First and foremost, what I want you to notice is that

the hotel was not obligated to take me to the airport, and neither was Arturo. This hotel typically doesn't make airport runs. Again, it wasn't Arturo's fault that my cab didn't show up. Nevertheless, he accepted the job of taking care of my problem. That's more than being responsible. That's being accountable: taking ownership of the situation, whether it be good or bad. That kind of experience built up my confidence in the team at Embassy Suites. You can bet it made me more likely to stay there again and encourage others to stay there as well.

- **Even when they are not your fault, problems encountered by customers and others who count on you may still be your obligation to solve.** The next time someone who's counting on you asks for help in dealing with a problem, take care of it, even if you know it's not your fault.

- **When there's a challenge, take full ownership of the situation.** Don't make excuses. Accept that you have a responsibility to find a path forward to the best possible outcome.

- **Personal accountability can create high levels of confidence in you and your team.** This kind of confidence leads to long-term loyalty.

GO THE EXTRA MILE

Amazing people deliver more than is expected.

IF YOU ASK ME, the most Amazing people of all are the ones who have the right attitude when it comes to going the extra mile. They're the ones who know just how big the payoff can be for exceeding expectations.

Most of us can recall a time when someone went not just a little but *way* beyond the call of duty for us. That kind of experience stands out, of course. When someone goes the extra mile on our behalf, we want to keep that person in our circle. Why? Because we prefer that experience to the experience of working with people who *never* go the extra mile or *barely* meet our expectations. At best, that's a *mediocre* experience.

Does that mean you have to go the extra mile each and every time you interact with someone? No. But what I do want is for you to recognize *opportunities* to do so.

Once you start noticing those situations where, with

just a little extra effort (sometimes very little effort), you can do more than expected. Doing so will put yourself and your team at a significant competitive advantage.

This advantage was encapsulated perfectly by Roger Staubach, the Hall of Fame Dallas Cowboys quarterback, who once said:

There are no traffic jams along the extra mile.

Going the extra mile is all about the baker's dozen, giving someone more than he or she expected. It's the extra time a salesperson spends helping you make the right selection. It's the customer support rep who takes an extra few minutes to ensure you have all your questions answered. It's the consultant who answers a call at 2:00 a.m. to help a client resolve an unexpected emergency. You get the idea.

A while back, I was talking to a client, Chris Cielewich, the vice president of sales at FLAVORx, about this very concept. FLAVORx manufactures a machine that takes terrible-tasting medications and flavors them in ways that kids love. Parents love this, too, because the kids are much more willing to take their medicine when it doesn't taste like medicine.

It turns out that when kids get to choose the flavor of their medicine, the percentage that actually takes the medication soars to around 90 percent. Sounds good so far, right? There is a catch, though, and here is where the concept of the extra mile comes into play.

If the customer asks for the FLAVORx, it takes the pharmacist an extra forty-five seconds to fill the prescription. Some pharmacies are so focused on productivity that they often don't want to take the extra forty-five seconds to do that, even if it creates a better customer experience.

Chris Cielewich conducted an experiment. He had three prescriptions to fill for his children and decided to go to three different pharmacies to see which pharmacist would recommend FLAVORx. With the kids in tow, he ventured out to fill the prescriptions. None of the pharmacists asked if the kids wanted their meds flavored. When Chris asked them to flavor the medicine, all three complied, but only one did so with a smile. The other two begrudgingly commented about how busy they were, obviously too busy to go the extra mile.

Here's my first question: If you're the parent, which pharmacist are you more likely to go back to?

And if you're the pharmacist, isn't it worth investing an extra forty-five seconds to ensure your customers are happier and will want to come back?

So what can you do to go the extra mile? Simple: *Notice* when the opportunity arises for you to give someone who's counting on you a little more than expected. That could be making an unexpected phone call to make sure the customer is happy. It could mean doing a little something extra for the work you do for a colleague. If you're a pharmacist, it could mean volunteering to ask a child whether he wants his medicine flavored as grape or sour apple. Whatever you do, though, remember this: you must never, ever make the other person feel as if he or she is an inconvenience when you go the extra mile.

- **Recognize opportunities to improve (sometimes dramatically) the quality of an experience with just a little extra effort.** Then execute.

- **You don't have to do something big to make a difference.** There are plenty of situations where something very small (such as an unexpected but well-timed e-mail message congratulating someone on a recent accomplishment) can improve an existing relationship.

- **Never, ever make the other person feel like an inconvenience.** Aim to deliver an exceptional experience every time, with no strings attached.

NEVER MAKE AN EXCUSE

Be a problem solver. Set up a plan of action that makes things better.

WHAT FOLLOWS IS A tale of two experiences.

Imagine you have booked a flight for an important business meeting. On the morning of the flight, you check the airline's website and learn that your plane is still scheduled to take off on time. Just before you leave for the airport, rain starts to fall. You get to the airport and you check the monitor, which indicates that your flight has been canceled. Your heart sinks as you realize you now need to rebook your flight. You stand in a long line to get to the ticket counter. You know from experience that you'll probably be waiting twenty to thirty minutes—or longer—before you get to the front. You call the airline on your mobile phone, hoping you will connect to a customer support representative sooner than you can get to the front of the line. Either way, *you're* the one who brings up the inconvenient reality that your flight has been canceled, *you're* the one who must explain your situation, and *you're* the one who must request help to set up a new reservation. Somewhere along the way, you might hear the airline employee say, "Most of the flights have been canceled. Every airline is dealing with this."

As you may have noticed, this experience culminates in an excuse. The little "dig" at the end about every airline having to deal with the problem is there to let you know the person behind the counter has a very good reason for not having gotten you out of the airport, on a plane, on time. That's not a great way to start the exchange.

An excuse is not the same thing as an explanation. It's just a little speech that makes someone—in this case, the airline employee—feel better. It's a rationalization that gets the other person off the hook. An explanation, by contrast, continues the conversation until it sets up some kind of accountable action.

Now let's take a look at a different example.

Just like you did in the first example, you check your flight online and see that it is listed as being on time. You get ready to go. It starts to rain. You get to the airport. You check the status board and you notice your flight has been canceled. You get in line. When you reach the front of the line, the person acknowledges that the bad weather has caused a lot of cancellations and apologizes for the inconvenience. Then he says, "I know I can't help you with the bad weather, but what I can do is help you get rebooked on another flight."

The second experience can be summed up in one word: *accountability*. It's an object lesson, not just for airlines, not just for our interactions with customers, but for our interactions with *everybody*.

When something goes wrong and someone who is counting on you has been let down, what's your first instinct? Is it to talk about how what happened wasn't really your fault? How what happened was unavoidable? How sorry you are for the person's inconvenience and trouble? If so, don't feel bad—those are all perfectly valid points of entry to the conversation—but if you stop there, all you've done is to make an excuse. You haven't broken through to the level of personal accountability, and that kind of accountability is where Amazement happens.

Don't stop at an excuse. Keep moving the conversation forward toward personal accountability.

- **Be proactive.** Reach out when you know there's a problem, rather than waiting for the other person to reach out to you.

- **Assume personal and/or organizational responsibility for what happens next.** Do this even if it's not your fault (and it probably isn't).

- **Don't make an excuse.** Explain what happened, and set up a plan of action or next step that supports the other person and makes his or her life easier.

KEY TAKEAWAYS FOR THE FOURTH HABIT: AMAZING PEOPLE TAKE PERSONAL RESPONSIBILITY

- If there are no downsides to giving the other person what he or she wants, assume you should do it.

- The purpose of your business—of any business—is to get and keep customers.

- Work from this assumption: It may or may not be our fault, but it definitely is our problem to solve.

- Never make the other person feel like an inconvenience. Go the extra mile. Deliver an exceptional experience every time, no strings attached.

- Don't make excuses. (Excuses stop short of offering a solution to the problem.) Make an explanation and then propose a next step that makes sense to both sides.

THE FIFTH HABIT:

AMAZING PEOPLE ARE AUTHENTIC

MEAN WHAT YOU SAY

Don't play games. Say what you mean and mean what you say.

HARRY ANDERSON IS THE actor best known for playing Judge Stone in the classic 1980s sitcom *Night Court*. Prior to that, he played a flimflam con man on *Cheers*. Anderson started his entertainment career as a magician, and to this day, he continues to pursue that passion. Years ago, I sent for a book that Anderson wrote about his act. The ad mentioned that I should indicate whether I wanted the book autographed. I did.

When the book arrived, the autograph on the opening page read:

Sincerely,

Harry Anderson

The signature was his, but above it, Anderson had rubber-stamped the word *Sincerely*.

You need to know a little about Anderson's career to understand how perfectly this gag fits his comic sensibility. There was always something slightly bogus about the personas Anderson adopted as an actor, something that made you wonder whether he really meant whatever line he was feeding you. He based his comic career on a convincing brand of insincerity. Whoever heard of a sincere con man? Even Judge Stone was a little off-center, a little implausible when he insisted on something.

Playing the role of an insincere, fast-talking, flimflam con artist can be a pretty good strategy if your goal is to get laughs from an audience. When it comes to getting results for others, though, you want to make sure you leave a different impression. You need to mean exactly what you say.

If you're in business, you simply can't be successful if your colleagues, your employees, and your customers don't believe what you're saying. You can't make people feel good about doing business with you if you're insincere.

Sincerity is all about trust—people trusting you, and you in turn creating a deeper sense of trust with other people. Those you work with should be able to trust every word that comes out of your mouth—and you should develop business alliances with people you trust implicitly.

Sincerity is about caring for the other person.

Sincerity is about loving what you do for a living, and

it's about helping others, through whatever it is that you do, to get what they want and need.

Sincerity creates confidence. And confidence may be the single most important reason that someone decides to do business with you.

Amazing people are sincere. They're authentic. They mean what they say. Conversely, they *don't* say anything they don't mean. Sincerity matters, because finding someone you can count on in this life—in business or anywhere else—is a very big deal.

Maybe the best way to understand what I'm getting at here is to share an experience many of us encounter every day, that of *insincerity*. I'm sure you've called for help in dealing with a problem—tech support, say, if you're having problems with a phone or computer—and heard the person respond with something like, "I'm sorry you're having difficulty."

Of course you have. We all have. Now, have you ever continued the conversation, gotten a little frustrated, and heard the person say exactly the same thing, "I'm sorry you're having difficulty," with exactly the same flat tonality? I'm betting you have. And then gotten really steamed at a particularly narrow-minded "problem solver," only to have the person say, for a third time and still with exactly the same intonation, "I'm sorry you're having difficulty."

If you have experienced that or anything like it, you know that the person's repetition of the scripted sentence, that supposedly expressed concern for you, conveyed exactly the opposite: a total disconnect with anything you had to say and a complete breakdown of trust in the relationship. That's inauthenticity.

A great actor and comedian like Harry Anderson could play insincerity for laughs. But when you're interacting in the business world with people who are counting on you, your job is to win trust, not laughs.

- **Say only what you mean.** If you make a commitment, make sure it's something you can stand behind.

- **Don't say what you don't mean.** If you don't know whether you can follow through on something, don't make the commitment.

- **Be as good as your word.** Remember that sincerity in the business world is about taking pride in what you do and standing behind it 100 percent.

GET TO "YES," GET TO "AND"

When there's a problem, show empathy and use creativity on your way to the resolution.

NOT LONG AGO, I was invited by Pegasystems, a software company based in Massachusetts, to attend their annual users' conference. The conference was all about customer relationship management (CRM). Some Amazing demonstrations and stories came out during the general and educational sessions, but one lesson in particular jumped out at me. It had to do with improvisational acting.

Perhaps you're wondering, *What does improv have to do with CRM and business?* According to Don Schuerman, Pegasystems's chief technology officer and vice president of product marketing, quite a lot. He shared an interesting lesson he learned firsthand from the world of improvisational acting.

Improvisational acting is a form of theater in which most or all of what happens onstage is created in the moment as it is performed. In other words, there isn't a script. One actor starts out with an idea and the other actors build from that. The actors have no idea where the scene will end. Fun for some, but more than a little scary for others. And as it relates to business, very relevant. We certainly don't know where a business conversation is going to go ahead of time. So how do we deal with that?

The answer, Don suggested, is improv. Improv demands that the performers be completely present in the moment. In other words, they must be fully engaged with each other and with the world of the scene. They must be authentic. That means no multitasking and no second-guessing. You're either in the scene 100 percent or you're not. For an improv scene to work, all the actors must be completely committed to their mutual interactions. They must be fully committed to the scene, and they must respect each other's choices.

If one person says a flying rabbit is dropping by for dinner, then that's the world of the scene. Period. Another actor can't say, "No, you're wrong. There's no such thing as flying rabbits."

Don's big lesson was about a technique called *Yes, And*. This really is the backbone of what improvisation is all about. First, you listen intently to the other actor. You acknowledge what he or she said and then add to the conversation. The acknowledgment is the *Yes*, and the addition is the *And*.

According to Don, not only does this make sense in the theatrical world, but it also brilliantly applies to business. While Don's focus is on the digital business world, this technique works for any type of interaction you have with your employees, colleagues, or customers. After listening to what the customer wants, acknowledge his or her point of view and deliver authentically—that's the *Yes*. Then add value based on your expertise—that's the *And*.

The next time someone comes to you with a problem or challenge, use the *Yes, And* model. Don't just throw out the "correct" response. Take a moment to acknowledge the other person's reality. Express complete commitment to the moment. Don't challenge what the other person has to say—that's the experience he or she is having. Be ready to say—and mean—things like, "If I were in your position, I'd probably feel exactly the same way." Or, "I get it." That's the *Yes* moment.

Then, having acknowledged the validity of the other person's experience, make a suggestion based on your own experience. Be ready to say—and mean—things like "What would happen if we..." or "Have you considered..." That's the *And* moment.

It's easy to forget: human beings need both the *Yes* moment and the *And* moment in order to feel connected to an exchange. That's true in the world of improv acting, and it's true in the world of business.

- **When someone comes to you with a problem or challenge, consider the *Yes, And* response model.** When you encounter a complaint, try to restate the other person's position, experience, or problem. That's a *Yes* moment. It shows full respect for the other person's perspective. Be present for him or her. Once you've done that, you can make a proposal for moving forward. That's the *And* moment.

- **Be fully present with people who are sharing a challenge or problem with you.** Don't let anyone or anything else distract you. Stay focused.

- **Use questions to defuse the situation when there's a problem.** Be ready to say—and mean—things like, "What would happen if we..." or "Have you considered..."

SHOW R-E-S-P-E-C-T

When you show respect, you're much more likely to get it in return.

EVEN IF YOU WEREN'T alive in 1968, when the song "Respect" first came out, the odds are pretty good that you've heard Aretha Franklin's hit song from that year and its unforgettable hook. In one of the catchiest lyrics in the history of pop music, Aretha spells out the title of the song, and demands that her man find out what respect really means to her.

I think one of the reasons that song has resonated with so many people for so long is that all of us feel a little bit like Aretha sometimes. We all want the people in our lives to understand what respect means to us.

One of the habits Amazing people follow is to acknowledge this universal, fundamentally human trait. Amazing people build up trust and connections in their relationships by offering authentic respect *before* they get it from others. In other words, when it comes to respect, Amazing people make the first move, and they do so sincerely.

In order for you to have the best and strongest business relationship with someone, respect has to be there. And it has to be authentic. Ultimately, respect is a two-way street. But the thing is, *we have to be willing to walk down that street first*. If we want respect from the other person, we have to be willing to deliver a message of respect before we get one. And we have to mean it, because sending people an inauthentic message of respect is worse than sending no message at all.

Sometimes people ask me, "Do I really have to show respect to someone who's not being respectful toward me? Suppose the person is being actively *disrespectful*?" Here's my answer: In any given situation, you don't have to respect the other person's *words* or *actions*. In fact, sometimes that's impossible. What you do have an obligation to respect, though, is the *potential for Amazement* that exists within the business relationship. And if you can't do that, then you probably need to rethink whether or not you want this relationship at all.

Respect begins with a conscious intention to treat the other person well, to listen, to be polite, and to express without any kind of prejudgment a sincere interest in the other person's situation and point of view.

In order to win respect, in order to get people to be respectful to you, you need to give evidence to them first that *you* respect them. So are you respectful to your customers, colleagues, and business contacts? Do they know it? Do they feel it? What are you doing to prove it?

Amazing people are constantly looking for ways to send an authentic message of respect in every business relationship—new, old, or somewhere in between.

- **Show common courtesy, no matter what.** Common courtesy is sometimes *uncommon* in the workplace and business settings. Don't let that happen. Never interrupt. Pay full attention during conversations. Call people the name that they want to be called. If you don't know, ask.

- **Listen actively before you share your own viewpoint or opinion.** If this doesn't come naturally—and sometimes it won't—try restating what you think you just heard the other person say, then ask a confirming question like, "Have I got that right?"

- **Be aware not only of the words you say but also the body language and tone of voice you use.** Even if you pick the "right" words to say, but you send nonverbal signals that tell the other person, "I don't respect you," your message will backfire.

PERSONALIZE IT

Make a memorable one-on-one connection.

ONE DAY, I WALKED into Total Hockey, a store in Saint Louis that sells hockey equipment. My regular salesperson, Kyle, was there to greet me. The conversation started out like this:

"Hello, Shep. Welcome back. Hope you are enjoying that new stick you bought last month and scoring lots of goals with it. The last time you were here you were looking at some new skates. Are you still interested in those? We have them in your size. Either way, you might also want to take a look at some new equipment we've just gotten in."

Kyle always seems to remember not only what I bought but also what I'm interested in, and he always gives me his full attention.

I had a similar experience when I logged into Amazon.com. You might be thinking it's difficult for a website to offer personalization, but because I've shopped there before, it seems as if they know me. The message from Amazon read, "Hello, Shep. Welcome back." The website had a picture of the book I looked at the last time I visited, and it recommended similar books to those I've purchased in the past.

Like Kyle, Amazon always seems to remember not only what I bought but also what I was interested in the last time I visited the website. It's really quite Amazing. Amazon manages to give me the same sort of customized, personalized attention that Kyle does.

My point is: They both create a great experience—an experience that doesn't feel superficial, artificial, or otherwise phony. An experience that feels, if you will, authentic. An experience based on a commitment to helping me make the best possible choices.

The key word there is *commitment*. Both Kyle and Amazon make me feel like I'm dealing with a friend, someone who knows me pretty well, and is personally committed to making sure I get exactly what I'm looking for. Kyle has personal authenticity down—I know he means exactly what he says. And if there's such a thing as digital authenticity, Amazon definitely has that figured out. *Both Kyle and Amazon are committed to personalizing the experience to the greatest degree possible.*

It would be wonderful to be able to say that every human being I run into is as committed to personalizing the exchange as Kyle is. But it wouldn't be true.

Not long ago, I called an electronics retailer I've

bought from many times before. A customer service rep answered and asked me, "What is your account number?" I didn't know my account number, so the operator asked, "Well, what's your phone number?" That seemed like a strange thing to ask, because I felt certain that every call center must surely be equipped with caller ID capability, but I followed the flow of the discussion and gave her my phone number. She then told me my account number and suggested I keep it for future reference. Then she asked what I was looking to buy, and I told her. "OK," she said. "I'll connect you with the appropriate department." The phone rang twice, and a new voice came on. Can you guess what this person's first question was? You guessed right: "What is your account number?"

That story gives you a perfect example of how *not* to personalize an exchange. Such stories are all too common. There are plenty of people I run into who don't recall anything at all about what we discussed last time and who don't have the slightest idea about what matters most in my world, even though I know I've discussed that with them. (And by the way, I'm not just talking about retailers here but any interaction you have with anyone.) They're not in the same league as Kyle. You could say that Kyle sets a high standard for that kind of commitment.

And by the same token, it would be nice to be able to say that every website I visit is as well organized, as carefully designed, and as focused on getting me exactly what matches my interests as Amazon's is. But that wouldn't be true either. You could say that Amazon sets the standard for personalization online. If anyone else does it better, I haven't seen it.

Take a lesson from Kyle and Amazon. Strive to personalize the relationship, whether the exchange is taking place in person or digitally. To the degree that you can, recall and make reference to the other person's past experiences with you and your team.

- **Personalize the relationship.** Care enough about the other person to keep track of what's happened between the two of you in the past. Make reference to the other person's choices and preferences. It shows that you care and helps create a stronger connection.

- **Keep good records. Create a database—either low tech or high tech.** If you need help when it comes to keeping track of what someone has done with you and/or your organization, write it down or record it in a software program. Sometimes that's better than just relying on your memory.

- **Leverage what you know about someone.** Use history to help that person make the best possible choices.

SHARE AN ATKINS MOMENT

Leave a positive, personal, authentic touch that others will remember and appreciate.

THE GREAT COUNTRY GUITARIST, vocalist, and record producer Chet Atkins—a major influence on artists as diverse as Chuck Berry, the Beatles, and Dolly Parton—was inducted into the Rock & Roll Hall of Fame posthumously in 2002. Before he passed, though, he gave us all a lesson in authenticity and Amazement.

A friend of mine, Kevin King, lives in Nashville and was friends with Atkins. Another buddy, Don "Mende" Mendenall, reached out to Kevin when he heard that the music legend was not long for this world. A lifelong Atkins fan, Mende heard that he was still willing to sign guitars for his fans. Mende wanted a guitar signed by his hero, and Kevin was the guy to get it done.

Mende went to a music store and bought an inexpensive guitar to send to Kevin. The guitar came back signed. But Kevin had more than a guitar and an autograph to pass along to Mende. He had a story.

"He didn't just sign your guitar," Kevin told Mende. "Even though he was really sick, he tuned it up and played it. I saw it and heard it."

"Wow," said Mende. "That's great."

"I asked him why he would go to the trouble," Kevin continued, "because I knew he wasn't really feeling all that well. He said he never signs a guitar that he hasn't actually played. He said he'd been doing that for years, and he wasn't about to change it now. He said that as long as he was going to personalize the guitar with an autograph, it only made sense to personalize it by actually playing the instrument. If someone's going to hang that guitar up on a wall somewhere, he wants it to be an instrument that doesn't just have *Chet Atkins* written on the outside but has a little Chet Atkins on the inside, too."

(By the way, as he strummed the guitar in question, Atkins said, "Kevin, this may just be the worst guitar I've ever played in my life.")

There's an eloquent lesson about sincerity in this story. Even on his deathbed, Atkins cared enough about what he was doing to make sure he did it personally. He was committed to the idea of leaving a little bit of what was unique about himself in his interactions with others.

I call this kind of interaction Atkins Authenticity. It's

all about adding the personal touch. What can you do to personalize your next business interaction with someone? What can you add to the exchange that no one else on earth could possibly add to it? How can you make sure it says you—inside and out? What you come up with doesn't need to take a whole lot of time, money, or effort, although it's fine if that's your style. What you add to personalize the relationship could be a little something extra that you add to an e-mail to a colleague, a card you leave on the desk of a new employee, or a special something for business associates sent out with holiday cards at the end of the year. Whatever it is, make sure it reflects who you are, what you love, and what you are committed to creating for others. Make sure it is authentic.

- **Live up to the standard of Atkins Authenticity.** If you touch it, make it better. Make it personal. Make it memorable.

- **Find new ways to impart a piece of yourself in important business relationships.** Add something that's distinctively you to the exchange, something that no one else could possibly add.

- **Find the joy.** Make sure that whatever you add to personalize an exchange, you add it with a sense of joy in what you do and gratitude for the opportunity to serve others.

KEY TAKEAWAYS FOR THE FIFTH HABIT: AMAZING PEOPLE ARE AUTHENTIC

- Say only what you mean. If you make a commitment, make sure it's something you can stand behind.

- Facing a complaint? Create a *Yes, And* moment by showing full respect and acknowledgment for the other person's experiences and perspective, then proposing a next step.

- Common courtesy and respect are sometimes uncommon in the world of business. Make sure it's your starting point.

- Connect your interactions with others, both in person and online, to positive past experiences with your organization.

- Find ways to personalize your most important business relationships.

AMAZING PEOPLE TURN MOMENTS OF MISERY INTO MOMENTS OF MAGIC

TURN IT AROUND

Do more than just solve the problem or complaint. Restore confidence.

RECENTLY, I HEARD A wonderful story about a family on vacation.

This family had been looking forward to their stay at a very nice hotel, but when they showed up, they found that there was a lot of construction going on at the hotel. Workers were walking around, there were a lot of signs up, and there was plenty of noise from all the hammering and drilling. As the father spoke to the front desk clerk who was there to check the family in, he mentioned that this really wasn't the experience he and his family had been expecting. He wasn't rude about it. He was just honest. He'd expected better.

By the way, this is what I call a Moment of Misery. I defined this concept earlier in the book (The Anatomy of Amazement). It's what happens when our expectations aren't met. We're disappointed. We get less than we antic-ipated, or maybe we have a complaint.

What I'd like you to notice about this story is what happened in response to that kind of complaint. The front desk clerk told the father he was very sorry about the noise and mess and would move him and his family to a floor without construction. But that's not all he did. In addition, he told the family he would upgrade them to a much nicer room.

Of course the whole family was delighted.

Here is the lesson: the front desk clerk didn't just fix the problem.

He restored confidence.

This habit of doing more than simply fixing problems is another consistent trait of Amazing people. They rec-ognize that Moments of Misery are really *opportunities to exceed the other person's expectations*. And they act on that opportunity.

Not only that, Amazing people know these opportuni-ties often come disguised as something else. Sometimes the other person might sound as if he or she is starting an argument or complaining. Guess what? Amazing people train themselves to recognize this situation for what it really is: the chance to restore trust by exceeding expecta-tions. And once they do, they strengthen the relationship.

This principle holds true in every business relationship.

If we're serious about delivering an Amazing experience to the people who are counting on us, we'll realize that it's our job to sidestep the argument, decline the chance to raise the tension, and look for ways we can get the trust level back up to where it needs to be. This takes practice. Practice is essential, and it pays off. Once we get into this habit, we will actually start looking forward to Moments of Misery, so we can turn the misery into Amazement.

What I love about this story is that it proves just how easy it can be to do that. I'm sure it looked to the father and the rest of the family as if the hotel went to extra effort and expense to make sure they got a nicer room. Actually, that's not what happened. That room was unoccupied. It hadn't been sold to anyone. It was going to go unused, so it wasn't going to cost the hotel any extra money to upgrade the family. It was actually a very easy business decision.

We all have more opportunities to restore trust in our relationships than we realize. This doesn't necessarily mean giving anything away—and it doesn't necessarily mean upgrading a family to a larger room. Many times, it is as simple as a smile, a positive attitude, and a quick response to fix what needs to be fixed. The only question is whether or not we're going to recognize these opportunities and act on them.

In this section of the book, you'll start to get better at recognizing opportunities to Amaze others—opportunities that come disguised as complaints or problems. These are going to come our way. There's no question about that. The only question is how we're going to respond.

- **Problems and complaints are inevitable.** Don't just fix the problem; restore the person's confidence in you and your team.

- **Forget about trying to make an excuse or win an argument.** Instead, recognize that Moments of Misery are really opportunities to Amaze.

- **Attitude matters.** When there is a problem or complaint, bear in mind that in many cases, all it takes to restore a person's confidence is the right attitude and a sense of urgency.

SEE PROBLEMS AS OPPORTUNITIES TO SHOW HOW GOOD YOU ARE

When something goes wrong, consider it your opportunity to hold on to the customer.

I RECENTLY PARTICIPATED IN a video project for a client. After we had spent a lot of time, money, and effort to complete the project, the director of the video crew discovered a mistake in our work. Unfortunately, it was a pretty big mistake. We had to reshoot several scenes, which meant we had to create the set exactly as it had been several days earlier. Because of this problem, I found out just how good this director really was.

While it was inconvenient for me to reshoot the scenes, it was both inconvenient and costly to the director. But he wanted it done right, and that was more important than convenience and sparing some extra expense. He was Amazing! We were able to deliver a high-quality video to the client, which is what I was initially after.

Sure, I'll use that director again. Sure, I'll recommend him if someone asks. But I will also go one better. I'll be his advocate. I'll tell everyone about him—even if they don't need to shoot a video. Why? Because he is Amazing, not only at what he does but also in how he treats people. Not just when things are going well, but when they aren't.

Let's be real for a second: Problems happen. That's reality. This director is one of my heroes and role models when it comes to problem resolution.

Let's look closely at what happened. Two days after the video shoot, the director called me with the bad news. They had lost six of the scenes we'd shot together. He felt terrible, because he knew that even though he was willing to come back and reshoot the scenes—at his expense—doing so would be a great inconvenience to me, as I would have to spend several more hours in front of the camera. My inconvenience seemed to bother him more than anything.

The moment he knew there was a problem, he informed me. He was truly sorry and made me feel that he would do just about anything to make it up to me. He assured me he could create a set that would be identical in every way—lighting, sound, everything—and that I had nothing to worry about.

He cared so much that by the time we finished our phone conversation, I felt bad that he felt so bad.

Isn't that the way it should be? Many of the people I do business with do what they are supposed to do, and when there is a problem, they take care of it. I appreciate them, but this time, it was different. There seemed to be an emotional hook. This person was not just doing the right thing but doing it with empathy, sympathy, concern, and care.

As previously mentioned, if you have a problem with a customer, many times all you have to do is take care of it quickly, with a sense of urgency and the right attitude, to regain the confidence of the customer. This director took that concept to another level.

Let's say that you have been doing business with some-one for twenty years and there has never been a problem. Then one day, it happens. Something goes wrong. There is a problem—a Moment of Misery. Whatever the problem is, I want you to consider this as your chance to shine. This is your opportunity to earn the right to keep the business.

I'm happy to pay my video director/producer for the work that he does. I have always had confidence in his work. And now I'm confident that he will stand behind his work—100 percent. Even more, if that were possible. He stakes his reputation on it. And that is enough for me to recommend him to everyone. His name is John Baker.

Most people who deal with him call him One Take Bake. I'll still call him that, even though this time we had to do a couple of extra takes.

- **Mistakes happen.** Remember that it's how you respond to the mistake that makes all the difference.

- **Whenever you know of a problem or an issue, don't hide it.** Tell the people who are counting on you as quickly as possible.

- **Have *more* concern for fixing the problem than the person you are serving has.** That's the best path back to Amazement.

FIND THE WHY

Determine exactly what happened, how it happened, why it happened, and what should happen next.

IT'S ALMOST A CLICHÉ to point out that we can and should "learn from our mistakes." Yet it's essential we remind ourselves of the importance of actually doing this when things go wrong. No matter how good we are, we're not going to be perfect, although it is a lofty and worthwhile goal. At any time, there can be issues, problems, and complaints. As you've seen, I call these negative issues Moments of Misery. Whenever something goes wrong, it's time for you to start looking for the WHY behind what happened. This is a consistent, predictable habit among Amazing people—in particular, among Amazing leaders.

I've compiled a list of questions you can and should ask yourself the next time something goes wrong (trust me, something will). My clients tell me that this list, which

I've written about in some of my articles, has helped them learn from experiences and prevent problems from happening in the future.

1. *What is the plan for handling this problem?* Identify an immediate solution which, delivered with the right attitude and a sense of urgency, will restore the person's confidence in you. If you haven't yet restored that confidence, what can you do to make sure that happens?

2. *Why did this happen in the first place?* Do some digging. Figure out why this issue arose.

3. *Has it happened before?* If it has, why did it happen again? Determine the real problem and what you can do to prevent, or at least minimize, the chances of it happening again.

4. *Can it happen again?* Is this the first time the problem or mistake has occurred? Find out what, if anything, could cause it to take place again.

5. *Can a new process keep it from happening again?* If there is a process that you can put in place to prevent the problem or mistake from recurring, implement it.

6. *Can you fix this before the person reaches out to you*

about it? This is extremely important. If you know the problem can happen, make sure you have a system in place to deal with it. Either fix it before the other person finds out, or let the other person know about the problem ahead of time. Be proactive.

7. *Who is involved in preventing it from happening (again)?* Identify who, specifically, is responsible for eliminating this problem or figuring out what has to be done if and when it arises.

8. *If this is a problem that doesn't happen often, if ever (i.e., a "freak occurrence"), what would we do differently in the same situation?* After the problem has been addressed and resolved, decide whether what you did was the best way to handle it. If there is a better way, find out what it is.

9. *Is there information we have now that we didn't have before this happened?* Look for new information or a new experience that will help you prevent it from happening again.

10. *What else did we learn from this?* Closely review all the answers to the above questions. You should have several insights into what happened, why it happened, and how you can prevent it from happening again.

Remember: These questions apply to everyone who is counting on you. That means internal customers as well as external customers.

It's just as important, by the way, is to conduct a similar "Find the Why" exercise when something wonderful happens—for instance, getting a letter or e-mail from a customer thanking you for doing a great job. In this situation, you'll want to ask questions such as:

1. *Why did this good thing happen?* Don't assume you know. Figure out what triggered the event.

2. *Has it happened before?* If so, find out when, how, and why.

3. *How likely is this to happen again if we don't do anything differently from what we're doing?* If the answer is "not that likely" or "we don't know," proceed to question 4.

4. *What is involved in making sure this good outcome happens more often?* If you can, set up a system that makes the positive outcome easier to repeat.

I'll share a true story with you of how this "Find the Why" approach can help you get to the root of a positive experience. At our company, we have a weekly staff meeting that always begins with team members sharing a Moment of Magic they created for a customer at some point during the past seven days. At the beginning of such a meeting, one of our team members reported that a certain customer had been "ecstatically happy" about a phone call the employee had returned. "That's great," I said. "Why did that happen?"

Over the next ten minutes or so, we worked our way through the relevant "Find the Why" questions that I've just shared with you. It turned out that the thing that had made this customer so excited about working with us was the speed with which we returned her calls. This is something we did automatically, but the discussion about this particular exchange made us realize two important things. First, the customer did not typically receive this level of service when dealing with others. In fact, she usually experienced long delays before her calls were returned. Second, we realized that although our record was good in this area, we had no formal standard for how quickly we aimed to return customer calls. As a result of this "Find the Why" discussion, we set such a standard: We always respond to calls within two business hours. That's a powerful target that has helped us to build better relationships with customers and others. We would never have set it without the "Find the Why" process.

When things go wrong, find out why.
When things go right, also find out why.

- **Ask yourself and your team the "Find the Why" questions when you know something has gone wrong—and when you know something has gone right.** For instance: Why did this happen in the first place? Has it happened in the past? Can it happen again?

- **Look for the patterns.** Bear in mind that something that goes wrong with one person can easily go wrong with many other people who are counting on you.

- **Set up a system.** Make sure it's one that will keep the problem from recurring, and set up systems that will ensure positive outcomes happen more often.

DON'T AVOID COMPLAINTS; MANAGE THEM

First, own the complaint. Then create a plan for moving forward.

ONE OF THE MAJOR reasons Moments of Misery happen is that complaints are simply mismanaged. That may sound like common sense, but unfortunately, it's not always as common as one would think. You've already learned (in The Anatomy of Amazement) you have a chance to not just fix the problem, but also restore confidence and create a Moment of Magic.

What's the difference between managing a complaint and mismanaging it? Consider this example. The other day, a friend of mine told me what happened when he phoned a delivery service to check on a package that was supposed to have shown up at his office.

"I gave the customer service rep the tracking number," my friend recalled. "It was an important legal document, something I needed for work, and I said so on the phone. I couldn't believe the response I got.

"After I told this person why I needed the documents, I could hear the guy punching information into his computer system, then hear him take a sip of coffee or something. There was a silence of about thirty seconds or so. When he came back to the conversation, he had a kind of combative tone to his voice as he said, 'Yes, it's been misdelivered, but you really need to keep this in perspective. You're dealing with an envelope that just has some papers in it. At least it wasn't anything urgent, like medicine for a hospital or something like that.'"

Now, where did that call *start* to go wrong? As you think about that, let's take a look at a second example.

A while back, I heard about someone who had tried to talk calmly and maturely to a work colleague about a project that was late. The colleague responded by saying that the person was being petty, "in view of everything else that's been going wrong in the company these days." Other people joined in, and the conversation quickly descended into a contest of "who's got it worst around here."

Now, here's another question: Where did *that* conversation start to go wrong?

If you haven't guessed already—although I bet you

have—I'll let you know that in each case, the person who was fielding the complaint decided to *avoid* the complaint by deflecting the issue and making excuses. This is mismanaging a complaint. It's even worse than making an excuse about the complaint. It borders on complete denial. And there is no way to transform a Moment of Misery if you are trying to change the subject. Instead, it's imperative that you manage the complaint, which starts by acknowledging what you hear the other person saying. You then respond to it authentically, even with empathy, as one human being to another, addressing the impact the situation has had on the other person, *whether you are personally responsible for that impact or not*, and then chart a way forward that makes sense to both sides.

If you can't do that—if you succumb to the temptation to change the subject, deflect the issue, or try to avoid what the other person is saying rather than dealing with it—then you're missing out on an opportunity to manage the complaint. The only position from which you can effectively manage a complaint is to own the complaint, even if it's not your fault. That's taking a position of full-on accountability.

- **Own the complaint.** There is no way to transform a Moment of Misery if you are trying to change the subject or deflect blame.

- **Humanize the exchange.** Acknowledge what you have heard with empathy, and consider the impact that the situation has had on the other individual.

- **Make viable suggestions for moving forward that have the potential to benefit both sides.** This is managing the complaint. It's the only way to get from a Moment of Misery to a Moment of Magic.

SPOT THE COMPETITION'S MOMENTS OF MISERY

Keep an eye out for an opportunity to gain a competitive advantage.

SO FAR, I'VE SHARED with you some of the best ways of making sure that you manage the transition for your colleague or customer from a Moment of Misery to a Moment of Magic—or even an Amazing experience. You also need to keep an eye out for—and be ready to respond to—the Moments of Misery that the competition sends your way. If you don't, you're letting your organization down, and who knows how many prospective customers and clients.

Here's a good example of what I mean. Lorraine went to a big hardware store she'd been going to for years. She was looking for something pretty basic—picket fence slats to repair the fence that surrounded her house.

With that goal in mind, Lorraine went into the lumber section. She got the last slats they had; in fact, she was still about a half-dozen short, and even the ones she'd picked up were too long. After a bit of searching, she eventually tracked down someone who worked in the lumber section of the store and asked whether there were any more picket fence slats. The answer was an abrupt and distracted "No!" Did the young man know where Lorraine could possibly find any more? Again, the answer was "No!" Well, could he help her out by trimming the slats she did have to the proper size? For the third time, Lorraine got the answer "No!"

This, in case you were wondering, was a textbook Moment of Misery. Notice that it doesn't have to incorporate anything that the company technically did "wrong." It can be (and often is) rooted in simple apathy.

Lorraine paid for the slats they had. She still needed more picket fence slats, though, so she headed over to another hardware store. The people there were considerably friendlier. When she explained what had happened, they not only pointed her right toward the slats she needed, but they also trimmed the slats she had bought from their competitor to the right size at no charge. Can you guess where Lorraine goes shopping for hardware now? (Good guess.)

Here's another example that illustrates the same principle. Juan, a web designer I know, answered the phone one day and found himself talking to a businessman in the midst of a crisis. Another Internet marketing company had built him a website that included many basic design mistakes. Prospects and customers were complaining about it. He asked if Juan could take a look and create a proposal for a new site, and he needed it quickly.

Juan said he'd be happy to. After just a little examination, he called the prospective client back. When he got him on the line, Juan said, "Yes, you're right. You do need a new website. But right now, let's get the one you have operational to the point where it's not hurting you. Let me help."

Juan ended up investing a couple of hours correcting the most obvious problems on the current website—the problems that were alienating customers and prospects. *He did not charge for that time.* After he had addressed the immediate crisis, the prospective client awarded Juan the business and became a client for life. It was obvious that Juan was just as interested in helping his client, if not even more so, than he was in winning his business.

Here's the moral to both stories: Whenever we find people the competition has underwhelmed or disappointed, or perhaps even a colleague who is looking for help but not getting it from the usual channels, we should seize the opportunity to show how helpful we can be. Look out for people's best interests. Take the high road. Show you're more interested in taking care of the problem than in making the sale. The sale is likely to follow.

- **The competition is eventually going to send you people who have suffered a Moment of Misery.** Your job is to understand that Moment of Misery and be ready to act in the best interests of the people the competition has let down.

- **You owe it to others to learn to recognize, and act effectively, on negative feedback that focuses on your competition.** Take consistent action on this.

- **Play for the long haul.** If you can turn the competition's Moment of Misery into a Moment of Magic, you can inspire not just gratitude but, potentially, long-term loyalty.

KEY TAKEAWAYS FOR THE SIXTH HABIT: AMAZING PEOPLE TURN MOMENTS OF MISERY INTO MOMENTS OF MAGIC

- Don't just fix the problem; restore the person's confidence in you and your team.

- Mistakes happen. Remember that it's how you respond to the mistake that makes all the difference.

- When something goes wrong, find the why. When something goes right, find the why, too.

- You can't transform a Moment of Misery into a Moment of Magic if you are changing the subject or deflecting blame.

- Learn to recognize a Moment of Misery from a competitor, and help the people they've let down.

AMAZING PEOPLE HABITUALLY FOCUS ON EXCELLENCE

MAKE EXCELLENCE A HABIT

It's what you do that matters, not what you know.

YOU'VE NOW SEEN SIX of the seven Amazement habits, and read plenty of examples of each of those six habits in action. Now it's time to look at the seventh habit, which may be the most challenging one of all, because it changes the way you look at yourself and your organization.

For many years, I've been talking to groups and individuals about the Amazement principles that we focused on earlier in this book, and I've noticed something interesting. After every speech, there's usually someone who comes up to me after the event is finished and says, "I could never do what you do." Meaning: I could never inspire someone. I could never share best practices about delivering a superior experience. I could never stand up in front of other people and spread the good word of Amazement.

Mastering the seventh habit means abandoning that excuse. You *can* do it. And if you execute on what I share with you next, you will.

Amazement, in the end, is active. It means giving up the right to say, "I could never do that." Whether you are the founder and CEO of the organization, the company's most recent hire, or someone who occupies a position somewhere in between, you really can master all seven of the habits and growth opportunities of truly Amazing individuals. The last, and probably the most important, of these opportunities involves *making a daily personal commitment to sustaining excellence in yourself and inspiring excellence in others.*

Yes, I'm talking about making Amazement a way of life, not just a once-in-a-while experience. I'm talking about making it the compass you use to get through the day, the week, the month, and the year, whether it looks like things are going well or it looks like things are going poorly. I'm talking about living Amazement all the time and engaging and inspiring others to do the same as a matter of daily habit.

The word *habit* is an important one, and it's one I want to challenge you to pay particularly close attention to in this final section of the book. Philosopher Will Durant[1]

---

1   http://blogs.umb.edu/quoteunquote/2012/05/08/
    its-a-much-more-effective-quotation-to-attribute-it-to-aristotle-rather-than-to-will-durant/

once said, "We are what we repeatedly do. Excellence, then, is not an act, but a habit."

The same is true of Amazement. Amazement is something you *do*, not something you know intellectually. It's something you live, every single day, as both a personal commitment and an organizational value. It can't just be something you read about.

In this part of the book, I will challenge you to create and reinforce the habit of putting the six Amazement principles I've shared with you into action—to the benefit of everyone who is lucky enough to become part of your network.

Maybe you're wondering, *How does Amazement become a habit?*

The answer is simple: Practice. Amazement becomes a habit if, and only if, you *practice* the principles of Amazement unwaveringly. Amazement becomes a habit when you do the necessary work up front to make Amazing interactions with others second nature. It becomes a habit once you go out on a limb and execute what you've read in the book—and what you're about to read. It becomes a habit once you commit to doing it on a daily basis. And that's what truly Amazing people do. They make Amazing interactions part of their daily routine. They practice.

Think of the actor who rehearsed his part so well that even the most unexpected distraction onstage can't faze him. Once the curtain goes up, he becomes one with the role he's playing. The transformation that takes place before he steps onstage is totally natural to him, and the audience never even notices it. They only notice the character. How is that possible? Practice, in the form of lots and lots of rehearsal.

Think of the professional golfer who practices a certain unlikely shot over and over again, so that when he's competing in a tournament, facing that same situation, the best response comes naturally. The crowd only sees the ball going into the hole, but the athlete and the caddy know how many years of repetitive practice went into that seemingly effortless shot.

Think of the jogger who gets up regularly at 5:00 a.m. to run her daily five miles. The first time she did it, do you think she was happy when she heard the alarm go off? Of course not. The first time, it felt like a much better idea to stay in bed. But with time, repetition, and some hard work, guess what happened? The situation turned around. Now, when the alarm goes off, she looks forward to the adrenaline rush of her morning run.

That's how it works with Amazement, too. At first, turning it into a habit feels inconvenient, uncomfortable, maybe even unnatural. But once you start in with some practice, once you begin implementing the principles, you find that it gets easier over time. And you even come to look forward to it.

- **It's not what you know about Amazement that matters.** It's how you *practice* Amazement that makes the difference.

- **Make the practice of Amazement part of your daily routine.** Share its guiding principles with others, both inside and outside your organization.

- **Maintaining an expectation of excellence, of constant, never-ending improvement, is one of the most inspiring habits of truly Amazing people.** They make a habit of focusing on excellence and inspire others as they do so. They make Amazing interactions part of their daily routine.

BE A STRAIGHT SHOOTER

Be known for your honesty and integrity. Level with people who count on you—all the time, no matter what.

THE MOST AMAZING PEOPLE I know are straight shooters all the time.

If you were to ask me to name the one predictable trait of Amazing people that is the most likely to make all the others easy to follow through on, it would be this one: tell the people who are counting on you the truth, the whole truth, and nothing but the truth. Level with people, even if it seems easier or advantageous not to. Be straightforward in your business dealings. (And in all your other dealings, for that matter. But this is a book about business, so that's what I'm going to focus on.)

You can't be Amazing to people who don't trust you. If you're not willing to level with people when it seems easier not to—if you're not willing to tell them what's really going on—you're not yet Amazing.

As an example, there are some people who exaggerate their qualifications and their capacities when a client or a prospective client calls and asks, "Hey, can you do X for us? Is X something you have a good track record with?"

It really isn't *shooting straight* to pretend that you've got expertise in something when you know you really don't. Think about how you would feel in this situation. A friend of mine hired someone to do a home remodeling job. He took a chance with a contractor who appeared to have the experience and said he could get the job done under budget and deadline. The contractor failed on both accounts and later admitted that this was a much bigger job than he had done in the past. He even ended up losing money on the job. How much easier would it have been for everyone if the contractor had passed on that job and let someone else more qualified take it on?

On occasion, a speaking or consulting project comes along that's outside my core area of expertise. Understand: I'm a customer service and customer experience expert. But every once in a while, a potential client calls or e-mails about something outside of my expertise. Maybe somebody wants me to come in and talk about sales. Or maybe someone wants me to train their team in time management.

Now, I could bring *some* insight and *some* experience to those kinds of assignments—but not a lot. I could do some of what they are asking me to, but I wouldn't really enjoy myself. And what's worse, I know I would be agreeing to deliver something that's really not one of my strengths and, at the same time, delivering a level of quality that I wouldn't be proud of.

Here's what I say to those requests: "Actually, although I would like to take it on, I won't. That kind of project really is not in my wheelhouse. There are a lot of other people who are really good at that. Would you like me to recommend one or two of them to you?"

Leveling with people—up to and including recommending the competition when you know it's in everyone's best interests for you to do so—makes everyone a winner. It's a much better business decision than trying to fake your way through something.

Sometimes it takes a little courage to admit that an opportunity isn't quite right for you. That you're not perfect. That you can't be all things to all people. But guess what? People will always appreciate it when you level with them. It's a sign of maturity and integrity. And it leaves the door open to future situations in which you really can add value. *Being a straight shooter always pays off, which is why it's worth practicing.*

Remember: People trust and respect straight shooters. Find someone who falls into this category in your own world, and make that person your role model.

- **Everyone wins when you level with the people who are counting on you. So practice doing that.** Don't fake it. Don't make something up. Specifically, don't exaggerate your experience, capacity, or ability.

- **Recognize the times when you are tempted to say things that are designed to please other people but aren't quite the truth.** Practice better responses.

- **Identify a straight shooter who has had a positive impact on your own life.** Use that person as a role model.

DO WHAT YOU SAY YOU'LL DO

Looking for a sure way to lose someone's confidence? Say you'll do something, then don't.

WE JUST LEARNED THE importance of making a habit of *shooting straight*, telling the truth. This is a follow-up to that concept. It is not just what you say that matters but also what you actually do. To be Amazing, you must be absolutely sure your actions match your words.

My friend Mike Ruwitch recently went to a baseball game with a group of friends and had a simple but powerful experience that illustrates this point. Mike told me: "In the second inning, the visiting team just hit a home run, so I figured it was the right time to order a beer. I stopped the beer vendor, who was walking down the aisle just then, and asked him for a couple of Bud Lights. He pulled out a business card and introduced himself as 'Buddy the Beer Man.' His card also said, 'Thank you for your business!' He also gave each of us a stick of bubblegum and promised to be back in the seventh inning when he would give us a chance to win a vintage baseball card if we answered his trivia question. We were delighted! We thought this guy was outstanding and told him to return often. We told him that he was our beer man, and we were going to wait and not buy from anyone else until he came back. Unfortunately, what started out to be a Moment of Magic turned into a Moment of Misery. Buddy never returned for the seventh inning. In fact, Buddy never even came back."

Mike was actually looking forward to that visit in the seventh inning, as well as visits throughout the game, but they never happened.

My point is: It *does* matter if you don't follow through on what you say, even with something as seemingly unimportant as selling a beer at a ball game. People notice. And they tell others.

Once you say you will do something, it's incumbent upon you to follow through. If you don't want to have to hold yourself accountable for doing something, *don't say you're going to do something or make a promise you can't or won't keep.* On the other hand, if you do make a commitment, do what Amazing people do: always follow through. If for some unforeseen reason you can't, then say so. That's where Buddy the Beer Man fell short. He made a great initial impression. He set an expectation. Then, he didn't follow through.

So why do we need to practice this? Because we live in a world where it's far, far too easy for people to say one thing and then do something else. For some (like Buddy), you can tell it's almost the default setting. We can't fall into that trap. We need to make a *conscious effort* to point ourselves the other way. If we're not careful, we may end up fooling ourselves into believing that there are no consequences for failing to do what we say we'll do. Amazing people know otherwise.

Amazing people know that following through on commitments, even small commitments, really does matter. They practice this all of the time. That's why others have confidence in them.

- **Follow through on what you say.** If you promise to do something, do it. If you create an expectation, at the minimum, meet it. At best, exceed it.

- **Communicate.** If you can't follow through, let the person know as soon as possible.

- **When in doubt, write it down.** If you need help keeping track of what you are personally accountable for following through on, enter your commitments into your daily calendar.

CULTIVATE THE LEADERSHIP MINDSET

Think like a leader, not like a follower.

ONE OF THE MOST important habits Amazing people develop is the habit of thinking like a leader.

They may not have the same title that the leader does, but that doesn't mean they can't develop the leadership mindset. They make a conscious choice to change the way they think. They stop thinking like employees.

This change in thinking doesn't happen overnight. If you've been trained—as many have, intentionally or not—to think like an employee on the job, you are likely to find thinking like a leader to be a bit of a struggle at first, which is good. If it were easy, it wouldn't be Amazing.

Below, you will find seven reminders that can help you build up the critical mental muscle I call the leadership mindset. If you pick one of the seven reminders to read out loud as you begin each working day and keep it in mind as the day progresses, you'll eventually find yourself practicing the leadership mindset more and more and spending less and less time in the follower mindset.

Here are seven big differences between the follower's mindset and the leader's mindset:

1. A leader doesn't act out of fear; instead, a leader inspires confidence.

2. Instead of focusing on not making a mistake, a leader focuses on adding value.

3. Instead of considering the rule book first, a leader considers the likely outcomes of his or her decisions first, *then* looks at the rule book—and knows which rules can be broken and when.

4. When a problem arises, a leader doesn't worry about who will be blamed; instead, a leader focuses on finding the right solution.

5. Instead of waiting for the current day to be over, a leader can't wait for the next day to begin.

6. Instead of spreading rumors, a leader spreads enthusiasm.

7. Instead of thinking in terms of job titles, a leader thinks in terms of relationships.

It's a matter of practice. If you make a point of coming back to this book regularly—say, every ninety days—to review the key takeaways, you'll develop the habits that turn *knowing* these seven differences into *living* the differences, each and every working day.

One of my favorite examples of someone who cultivated the leadership mindset was Lisa, a college intern who worked at our company one summer. I came in to work one morning and noticed that someone had alphabetized all the books in our customer service library by the author's last name. It turned out Lisa had done this—without anyone asking her to. A week or so later, I learned that Lisa had created a special reporting system that allowed us to track and analyze our social media numbers more effectively. Again, she had done this entirely on her own; no one had suggested that she take the time to create this solution. It benefited the entire team and improved multiple workplace relationships. These are examples of how Lisa found solutions and added value to everything she touched. She showed all of us what the leadership mindset looked like in action.

- **Know the difference between a leader and a follower.** Followers focus on getting through the day unscathed and following the rules. Leaders focus on adding value, spreading enthusiasm, and improving relationships.

- **Make leadership thinking a habit.** If you've been trained, as many have, to think like a follower on the job—for instance, by thinking about staying out of trouble rather than adding value—you are likely to find thinking like a leader to be a bit of a struggle at first. Don't give up. This type of thinking takes practice and repetition. That's what makes it a habit.

- **Focus on being a leader.** Strengthen your mental "leadership muscle" by focusing your attention, at the beginning of the working day, on the differences between the leadership mindset and the follower mindset.

SWEEP LIKE BEETHOVEN PLAYS PIANO

Make a lifetime commitment to Amazement.

WHEN I TALK ABOUT the seven Amazement habits, most people get it instantly.

But let's be honest. We all run into obstacles. We all need encouragement from time to time. And we are all at risk for having the kind of day when we wonder whether Amazement—a continuous commitment to a level of quality in our business relationships that exceeds expectations—is really worth the effort. Let me arm you ahead of time with three inspirational thoughts to keep you going. Committing to a rigorous course of ongoing improvement in the seven habits I've shared with you in this book is worth doing because it delivers:

1. A clear competitive advantage for you and your organization

A constant, never-ending commitment to quality, to excellence, to Amazement, in all of your (and your team's) interactions instantly sets your organization apart from the competition. If all other factors are equal, and very often they are, something has to tip the scales in your favor when the customer is choosing whom to do business with. The quality of a relationship where people *know they can trust you and your team* will consistently make the critical difference in the customer's decision to buy your company's product or service—and keep buying it.

2. A clear career advantage for you

Once you make your way into the circle of someone who knows you're Amazing, opportunities have a way of opening up for you. That translates to a long-term career advantage that is hard to beat. The quality of your relationships will tip the scale in your favor. It makes it easier for people to recommend you, send you referrals, and do business with you.

3. Personal fulfillment

Perhaps the best and most compelling reason of all to put what you've read into rigorous practice is that it's *much more fulfilling to aspire to excellence than it is to settle for mediocrity.* Aspiring to excellence makes us feel better about what we are doing and what we were sent here to do. I believe people are happier when they have a calling in life. The happiest ones I've met do. And I count myself among them. I'd like to think that you could be lucky, too—that what I've shared with you in these pages can inspire you to become one of those people who focuses relentlessly on Amazement, not as a short-term solution to a problem but as a long-term calling—as a way of living, day after day. That kind of life is a life worth living, and I do hope it's the kind of life you choose for yourself.

It doesn't matter whether you are the CEO of your organization, or you've just been hired at the entry level. Either way, if you're inspired to follow the example of Amazing people, you're going to want to do your best. Martin Luther King Jr. made a powerful point about the power of an Amazing life—a life well lived and lived to the fullest by the individual blessed to live it—when he said:

> *If a man is called to be a street sweeper, he should sweep streets even as a Michelangelo painted, or Beethoven com-*

*posed music, or Shakespeare wrote poetry. He should
sweep streets so well that all the hosts of heaven and earth
will pause to say, "Here lived a great street sweeper who
did his job well."*

Amazement is not an act. It's a habit. Here's to doing
the job well for its own sake and to the benefit of all those
our work affects.

- **An Amazing life is a life well lived.** This is a life
  lived to the fullest by the individual blessed to live it.

- **Do your job well for its own sake—no matter
  what your calling in life.** This will deliver significant career advantages, as well as a deep sense of
  personal fulfillment.

- **Amazement is not an act. It's a habit.** Get into the
  habit of living the Amazement principles, each and
  every day—not just reading or memorizing them.

KEY TAKEAWAYS FOR THE SEVENTH HABIT: AMAZING PEOPLE HABITUALLY FOCUS ON EXCELLENCE

- Amazement means making a daily personal commitment to sustaining excellence in yourself and inspiring
  excellence in others.

- Everyone wins when you level with the people who are counting on you. So practice Amazing behaviors regularly.

- Make a habit of following through on what you say. If you create an expectation, meet it, or even better, exceed it.

- When there's a problem, listen. Focus on the relationship first, not just the rules.

- Employees focus on getting through the day unscathed by just following rules. Leaders focus on adding value, spreading enthusiasm, and improving relationships.

- Committing to excellence delivers a clear competitive advantage to your organization, a clear career advantage for you, and a sense of personal fulfillment.

EPILOGUE

MEDIOCRITY IS THE ENEMY OF AMAZING

Take a stand against mediocrity. Adopt a mindset of always being above average, always growing and improving, always being Amazing.

EVERYTHING YOU'VE READ IN this book has pointed you toward the idea of *thinking ahead* on behalf of your most important business relationships, by planning more effectively, by taking personal responsibility, and by taking action to keep little problems from becoming big problems. Unfortunately, this is not always how people do business.

The way some people do business is *not* to think ahead on behalf of those who are counting on them, *not* to look around corners, *not* to deal with problems until they get big enough to become a "priority," at which point they decide it's time to swing into action. That's what often happens.

That's known as mediocrity, and mediocrity is, unfortunately, what usually happens in business relationships and all relationships. Mediocrity is doing the bare minimum necessary to get by. Mediocrity is about average or satisfactory. Mediocrity is familiar to all of us, and we need to recognize that it's the sworn enemy of Amazing.

As I close this book, let me urge you to remember that a culture of mediocrity will sabotage any attempt you make to create and live by a culture of Amazement.

It takes a whole new mindset to rise above the standard of mediocrity. It takes a new way of looking at the people in your circle. It takes a commitment to create a very different kind of interaction, one based on finding the best possible outcome for both sides.

Mediocre interactions don't do that. And they don't leave people Amazed. They don't make people go out of their way to give you referrals, stay in contact with you, and resolve to keep working with you, month after month and year after year. All of that is the result of an attitude of Amazement, and it's impossible in a mindset of mediocrity.

At the end of the day, being Amazing means challenging the status quo. We can do that by making an ongoing commitment to improve the experiences we deliver and by proactively improving the quality of our thinking, our products, and our personal service. This is a transformative, ongoing way of looking at the world. It means never being satisfied with "satisfactory" or "average."

Now, I'm not suggesting that you should try to transform all your processes overnight. But I am suggesting that you can and should point yourself and (to the degree that you can) your organization toward the due north of continuous improvement and continuous progress toward Amazement, each and every day. If you commit to making a little measurable improvement each day in some area that positively affects your most important relationships, you can rest assured that you will steer clear of the mindset of mediocrity and point yourself toward Amazement.

Join the ranks of those who are headed in the right direction, trying their best to be measurably better than they were yesterday, every day. Join the ranks of the people who are fully committed to making sure customers and others who are counting on them have somebody who is willing to look out for them no matter what. If you do that, you will have laid the foundation of Amazement.

- **Don't accept mediocrity.** Average is the default setting. Being Amazing requires that we take on personal responsibility for the outcomes people are likely to receive from us.

- **Make Amazement a way of life.** Do what you can with what you have right now to raise the level of quality that you deliver to others.

- **Lay the foundation of Amazement.** Look out for the people who are counting on you.

BE AMAZING CHECKLIST

So now you know how to be Amazing, but it's not enough to just know how to be Amazing. You must be Amazing. It's something you must do every day, something that needs to be practiced.

This section is a checklist that will help you gauge your current level of Amazement. Look through the list, and check off the Amazement habits you currently practice. (By "currently practice" I mean that you live these habits instinctively and without hesitation.) The goal of this exercise is to find opportunities for you to improve.

☐ **Show gratitude:** Amazing people appreciate what they have and express appreciation to others.

☐ **Show up ready to Amaze:** Amazement is all about showing up at the top of your game every time.

☐ **Work on Lombardi Time:** Set a higher standard, and never be late for the people who count on you.

☐ **Remember you're always on stage:** When it comes to Amazement, make a habit of aiming high, because people are watching.

☐ **Look beyond the clock:** You represent the company whether you're clocked in or not, so act like it.

☐ **Enter the Anti-No Zone:** Imagine, and live in, a world where the word *no* isn't the first option.

☐ **Be proactive:** Instead of waiting for things to happen, make them happen.

☐ **Think ahead:** Anticipate what's next, so you can stay a step ahead.

☐ **Create a predictable positive experience:** Inconsistency lowers the level of trust in relationships and undermines the loyalty of the person who has chosen to work with us.

☐ **Think outside the rule book:** Think of the relationship before you start reciting the rule book.

☐ **Stay a step ahead:** Create a process that solves problems before others find out that there was a problem.

☐ **Ask directly for feedback:** The person who doesn't think that he or she needs constructive criticism is the one who needs it the most.

☐ **Look past the honeymoon:** Make sure you meet the expectations of the people who count on you today and tomorrow, too.

- ☐ **Rate yourself:** You can't improve what you don't measure.

- ☐ **Fulfill the promise:** Create and keep your personal brand promise.

- ☐ **Commit to constant, never-ending improvement:** Always look for new ways to Amaze.

- ☐ **Own it! Take personal responsibility:** Make sure that issues stop with you, and never duck responsibility.

- ☐ **A common purpose:** Know the purpose of every business—to keep customers.

- ☐ **It's not my fault, but now it's my problem:** Step up when things go wrong, because even though it may not be your fault, it is your opportunity to Amaze.

- ☐ **Go the extra mile:** Amazing people deliver more than is expected.

- ☐ **Never make an excuse:** Instead of making an excuse, set up a plan of action that makes things better.

- ☐ **Mean what you say:** Say what you mean and mean what you say.

☐ **Get to "Yes," get to "And":** When there's a problem, show empathy and be creative to resolve it.

☐ **Show R-E-S-P-E-C-T:** When you show it, you're more likely to get it in return.

☐ **Personalize it:** Know whom you're talking to, and use that to create a better experience.

☐ **Share an Atkins Moment:** Give what you deliver a positive, personal, and authentic touch. Others will remember and appreciate it.

☐ **Turn it around:** Go beyond solving problems or complaints into restoring confidence.

☐ **See problems as opportunities to show how good you are:** Mistakes happen. Use them to show how an Amazing person deals with mistakes.

☐ **Find the why:** Good or bad, learn exactly what happened, how it happened, why it happened, and what should happen next.

☐ **Don't avoid complaints. Manage them:** Own the complaint, then create a plan for moving forward.

☐ **Spot the competition's Moments of Misery:** When

a customer comes to you with a Moment of Misery from a competitor, use it to your advantage.

☐ **Make excellence a habit:** Being Amazing is about what you do, not what you know.

☐ **Be a straight shooter:** Be known for being honest and having integrity.

☐ **Do what you say you'll do:** If you say you're going to do something but you don't, you will lose people's confidence.

☐ **Cultivate a leadership mindset:** Think like a leader, not a follower.

☐ **Sweep like Beethoven plays piano:** Make a lifetime commitment to Amazement.

☐ **Mediocrity is the enemy of Amazing:** Take a stand against mediocrity. Adapt a mindset of always being above average, always being Amazing.

New habits take time. If you identify ways to be more Amazing and practice them, it won't be long until they become a habit. And one of the most important habits is to "Commit to constant, never-ending improvement." With that habit in mind, I hope you will be inspired to go beyond the habits listed in this book. Come up with some of your own. Once you do, add them to the book by writing them down in the space provided below.

ACKNOWLEDGMENTS

IN THE PROLOGUE, WHICH focused on the habit of showing gratitude, I recognized and acknowledged you, the reader. If you didn't read my books, I wouldn't write them. So once again, thank you!

There are plenty of people who helped bring this book to fruition, and I am grateful to all of them. Once this book started to go from a concept in my head to a manuscript, there were many people involved who deserve to be acknowledged and thanked. My rough draft was very rough; I almost threw it away. Then I reached out to my friends at Cara Wordsmith, Ltd. Their ideas and suggestions helped me get to a manuscript that made me say, "Yes, it's finally a book!" The next step was to edit and proofread, and I want to give a shout-out to the newest member of the team at Shepard Presentations, Mark Benton, whom we refer to as Mark the Intern. His first responsibility as a summer intern at Shepard Presentations was to proofread the manuscript. From there, it went to Linda Read, who has helped edit many of my articles and special reports and worked with me on my last book, *Amaze Every Customer Every Time*. She is the one who crosses the t's and dots the i's. At that point, it was ready to be published. The team at Book In A Box took the finished manuscript to the published work you hold in your hands (or are reading on your screen), and they did a great job.

Finally, I'd like to thank Cindy Hyken, my wife and my best promoter. Thanks for the support, the honest feedback, and for everything else you do to make my life—dare I say—Amazing!

AMAZING Customer Service is a habit...

When is comes to creating and delivering amazing service, it's everyone's job, regardless of their position. It's about adopting the right mindset and having the right attitude about your customers, both internal and external.

Shepard Virtual Training -
Bringing our best customer service training direct to you and your team.

Customer service expert and New York Times best-selling author Shep Hyken, has created some of the best online customer service training available. Through this innovative web-based training and communications platform, **Shepard Virtual Training** presents full motion, interactive modules that teach you (or your entire team) the essential techniques and tactics needed to make every customer service experience AMAZING!

24/7 online access allows you to train on your own desktop, laptop,or tablet whenever it's most convenient.

Creating an *AMAZING* customer experience... that's what it's all about.

Enroll today at www.ShepardVirtualTraining.com or for more information call 314.692.2200
Group Licenses available at substantial discounts.

ABOUT THE AUTHOR

SHEP HYKEN is a customer service and experience expert and the Chief Amazement Officer of Shepard Presentations. He is the *New York Times* and *Wall Street Journal* bestselling author of *Moments of Magic*, *The Loyal Customer*, *The Cult of the Customer*, *The Amazement Revolution*, and *Amaze Every Customer Every Time*. His articles have appeared in hundreds of publications, and he has been inducted into the National Speakers Association Hall of Fame for lifetime achievement in the professional speaking industry. Shep is also the creator of The Customer Focus, a customer service training program that helps clients develop a culture and loyalty mindset.

For more information visit www.Hyken.com

A special gift for you!

As a special thank you, be sure to visit
www.BeAmazingOrGoHome.com
for your free gift!

(And you'll be happy you did!)

And don't forget to follow me:

ShepHykenSpeaker ShepHyken @hyken ShepHyken